FROM THE RAPTURE UNTIL

Randy H. Edwards

EVER-READ PUBLISHING CO.
1675 Pipers Gap Rd.
Mount Airy, NC 27030

*To Order Use Above Address
or Call (919) 786-4805*

Copyright 1993
Randy H. Edwards

Published by EVER-READ PUBLISHING CO.
1675 Pipers Gap Road
Mount Airy, NC 27030

Library of Congress Cataloging in
Publication Data

Library of Congress Catalog Card Number: 93-70812

ISBN - 0-9635986-7-8

DEDICATION

This book is lovingly dedicated to my family. They have brought great joy to my life through their love, their fellowship and their prayers. This family is Sandy, Joshua, Charity and all the people of Faith Baptist Church in Mount Airy, North Carolina.

TABLE OF CONTENTS

INTRODUCTION

What publication could have a more important purpose than to help the reader understand events of the end time from The Rapture - Until?

This book is designed to help you understand scriptures associated with prophetic events and to encourage you to study scriptures printed within the text as well as the entire Bible.

This book has several purposes. One of which is to tell of the wonderful promises of those who have been saved by God's amazing grace. It also reveals events of the end time and warns of what will happen to those who have never accepted Jesus as their Savior.

Rather than delay further, prepare yourself for a most interesting trip into the future of mankind through the prophetic scriptures which are presented in this book.

And, if you are not one of those ready to claim the promises of those who are saved, it is hoped these pages will help you make the decision to make the Lord your Savior.

The Prophecy Time Line

——— Follows the Saved.
- - - - Follows the Lost.

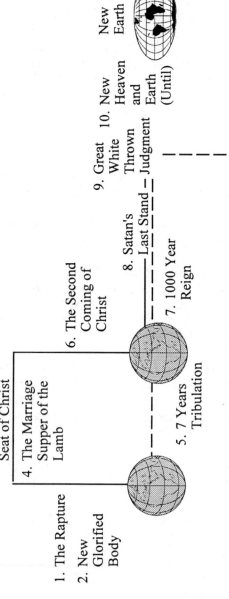

1. The Rapture
2. New Glorified Body
3. The Judgment Seat of Christ
4. The Marriage Supper of the Lamb
5. 7 Years Tribulation
6. The Second Coming of Christ
7. 1000 Year Reign
8. Satan's Last Stand — Judgment
9. Great White Thrown Judgment
10. New Heaven and Earth (Until)

New Earth

New Jersulam

Eternal Lake of Fire

This time line is to help you understand when prophecy events take place and the sequence of the events.

EXPLANATION OF THE PROPHECY TIME LINE

This is to give you a general idea of the order of prophetical events. Truly the next great event to happen is the Rapture of the saved. At the Rapture the saved will be given new glorified bodies. If you will follow the unbroken line (_____), you will find the saved then go to the Judgment Seat of Christ followed by the Marriage Supper of the Lamb.

The broken line (-----) shows that the unsaved are left on earth to go through the Tribulation during this time. After the Marriage Supper the saved then return to the earth with Christ during the Second Coming. The Second Coming is followed by the 1000 Year or Millennial Reign. Satan is then loosed for a little season which results in Satan's Last Stand. This is followed by the Great White Throne Judgment which leads us to the New Heaven and the New Earth which is the eternal state of the believers. This results in the final chapter of this book which we call "UNTIL".

THE RAPTURE

As we begin this lesson we want to make sure you understand that the Rapture of the church and the second coming of the Lord Jesus Christ are two separate events. At the Rapture, Jesus will descend to a point above the earth and call all believers to Him. At the second coming, the Lord will come all the way down to the earth. These two events are separated by a time span of seven years and should not be taught as one event together. Learning the prophecy time chart that is provided for you in this book will be a great benefit for you.

I.   What is the Rapture?

    A.   The word Rapture is best defined as the state of being transported from one place to another.

    B.   And in the Rapture that we are learning about, that transportation is from this earth to meet the Lord in the air. Several passages of scripture point this out.

        I Thessalonians 4:14–18 For if we believe that Jesus died and rose again, even so them also which sleep in Jesus will God bring with him. [15] For this we say unto you by the word of the Lord, that we which are alive and remain unto the coming of the Lord shall not prevent them which are asleep. [16] For the Lord himself shall

9

descend from heaven with a shout, with the voice of the archangel, and the trump of God: and the dead in Christ shall rise first: [17] Then we which are alive and remain shall be caught up together with them in the clouds, to meet the Lord in the air: and so shall we ever be with the Lord. [18] Wherefore comfort one another with these words.

I Corinthians 15:51-53 Behold, I shew you a mystery; We shall not all sleep, but we shall all be changed. [52] In a moment, in the twinkling of an eye, at the last trump: for the trumpet shall sound, and the dead shall be raised incorruptible, and we shall be changed. [53] For this corruptible must put on incorruption, and this mortal must put on immortality.

C. According to these verses Jesus will descend from Heaven to a point just above the earth and will call for the church. The saved people will, in a twinkling of an eye, go up to meet him.

II. Who will be involved in the Rapture?

A. The first person that will be involved is the Lord Jesus Christ.

I Thessalonians 4:16   For the Lord himself shall descend from heaven with a shout, ...

My friend, isn't it exciting that the very one that loves us so much is the one that will be coming for us. Not an angel or some special servant, but Jesus will be coming with a shout.

B.   Another participant in the Rapture will be the archangel.

I Thessalonians 4:16   ... with the voice of the archangel, ...

The name of this archangel could very well be Michael. The Bible reveals that Michael is an archangel.

Jude 9   Yet Michael the archangel, when contending with the devil he disputed about the body of Moses,...

And we also know from the scriptures that Michael will be very involved in Bible prophecy.

Daniel 12:1   And at that time shall Michael stand up, the great prince which standeth for the children of thy people: and there shall be a time of trouble, such as never was since there was a nation even to that same time: and at that

11

time thy people shall be delivered, every one that shall be found written in the book.

C. The largest group involved in the Rapture will be all the Christians that are dead.

I Thessalonians 4:16 ... and the dead in Christ shall rise first:

I Corinthians 15:52 .... and the dead shall be raised incorruptible, and we shall be changed.

The bodies of those believers that have already died will be raised up and transformed into an incorruptible, immortal and glorified body. This does not mean that they are not in Heaven now. Those that have died in Christ are in Heaven now, that is their soul and spirit is in heaven.

II Corinthians 5:8 We are confident, I say, and willing rather to be absent from the body, and to be present with the Lord.

Jesus will bring forth their former bodies, change the former bodies to a glorified one, and then reunite the soul and spirit with the new glorified body.

12

Job 19:25-26 For I know that my Redeemer liveth, and that he shall stand at the latter day upon the earth: [26] and though after my skin worms destroy this body, yet in my flesh shall I see God.

These will be caught up together with the other believers that are living at the time of the Rapture to meet the Lord in the air.

D.   The next group of people that will be involved in the Rapture are those Christians that will be alive when the Rapture happens.

I Thessalonians 4:17   Then we which are alive and remain shall be caught up together with them in the clouds, to meet the Lord in the air; and so shall we ever be with the Lord.

I Corinthians 15:51   Behold, I show you a mystery: We shall not all sleep, but we shall all be changed.

Each one who is saved will, in a blink of an eye, be transformed into an incorruptible, immortal and glorified body.   They will also be caught up from this earth with those deceased believers

13

to meet the Lord in the air. Nothing will prevent this from happening. Not a pressing engagement, a job, sickness or even the gravity of this earth. When the Lord calls, we will be changed and go to meet him faster than you can blink your eye.

E.   The last group of people involved in the Rapture are sometimes a little harder to identify. I believe this group will consist of all the babies, small children, and even those with mental problems that have not come to the age of knowing right from wrong.

III. When will the Rapture take place?

A.   I truly believe this is the next great event in God's prophetic calendar. Some people believe the Rapture could happen in the middle or at the end of the tribulation period. We will study this period in another lesson. Right now, we want to show that the Rapture will take place before the tribulation period.

B.   The tribulation period will be a time when wrath will be poured out upon the earth. The people that are saved are not the subjects of this wrath.

Romans 5:9 Much more then, being now justified by his blood, we shall be saved from wrath through him.

I Thessalonians 1:10 And to wait for his Son from heaven, whom he raised from the dead, even Jesus, which delivered us from the wrath to come.

I Thessalonians 5:9 For God hath not appointed us to wrath, but to obtain salvation by our Lord Jesus Christ,

This fact is also proven by the angels transporting Lot and his family out of Sodom before the wrath came.

Genesis 19:15-16 And when the morning arose, then the angels hastened Lot saying Arise, take thy wife, and thy two daughters, which are here; lest thou be consumed in the iniquity of the city. [16] And while he lingered, the men laid hold upon his hand, and upon the hand of his wife, and upon the hand of his two daughters; the Lord being merciful unto him: and they brought him forth, and set him without the city.

C.   Also supporting the fact that the Rapture will happen before the tribulation period is that in scripture concerning the Tribulation there is no mention of the church. Up to Revelation Chapter 6, the church is mentioned many times.

Notice just a few of these verses.

Revelation 2:7 He that hath an ear, let him hear what the spirit saith unto the churches; ...

Revelation 2:11 He that hath an ear, let him hear what the spirit saith unto the churches; ...

Revelation 2:17 He that hath an ear, let him hear what the spirit saith unto the churches; ...

These are just a few of the many times that the church is mentioned in the first few chapters of Revelation. Then from Revelation Chapter 6 through Chapter 19 there is no mention of the church at all. These chapters are concerning the tribulation period. Notice this verse from that section of scripture concerning the tribulation period.

Revelation 13:9 If any man have an ear, let him hear.

Notice there is no mention of the church. Truly this is the next great event. The Rapture can actually take place any time now. What an exciting time we are living in.

IV. What will be the results of the Rapture?

A. All those who have accepted Christ as Savior will be gone from the face of the earth. They will be reunited with friends and loved ones that have already gone to be with the Lord.

B. All of the babies and small children along with those who have mental problems and have never come to the age of knowing right from wrong will also go up in the Rapture.

C. There will be a time of havoc on the earth. Can you imagine the scene at the hospitals, schools, restaurants, malls and our highways as thousands of people disappear from the earth. These people will be searched for, just as they looked for Enoch who is a foreshadow of the Rapture.

Hebrews 11:5 By faith Enoch was translated that he should not see death; and was not

found, because God had translated him:

There was also a lot of concern when Elijah was caught away; he, too, is a foreshadow of the Rapture.

II Kings 2:16-17 And they said unto him, Behold now, there be with thy servants fifty strong men; let them go, we pray thee, and seek thy master: lest peradventure the Spirit of the Lord hath taken him up, and cast him upon some mountain or into some valley. And he said, Ye shall not send. [17] And when they urged him till he was ashamed, he said, Send. They sent therefore fifty men; and they sought three days, but found him not.

D.   There also should be results of the Rapture present right now in our lives. One of which is thoughts of the Rapture should bring comfort to us.

I Thessalonians 4:18 Wherefore comfort one another with these words.

It should also result in our trying every day to live as close to the Lord as we can.

I John 3:2-3 Beloved, now are we the sons of God, and it doth

not yet appear what we shall be: but we know that, when he shall appear, we shall be like him; for we shall see him as he is. [3] And every man that hath this hope in him purifieth himself, even as he is pure.

If we truly consider the frailty of life, and the fact that the Rapture could happen any time, it will result in us trying to win souls. No one is ever promised tomorrow to get right with the Lord.

James 4:14 Whereas ye know not what shall be on the morrow. For what is your life? It is even a vapor, that appeareth for a little time, and then vanisheth away.

OUR NEW GLORIFIED BODY

I. Will be like the body of Christ.

II. Will be a body of flesh and bone.

III. Will be recognizable.

IV. Will be a body in which the spirit dominates.

V. Will be unlimited by time, space or even gravity.

VI. Will be an eternal body.

VII. Will be a glorious body.

One of the most beautiful and exciting facts of salvation is that one day the saved will have a new glorified body. We are a triune being made up of the body, the soul, and the spirit. When we get saved, our soul is saved from hell. A new spirit is put within, but the body is still the same. However, at the Rapture of the church, our body will be changed.

> **I Corinthians 15:51-56 Behold I shew you a mystery; We shall not all sleep, but we shall all be changed, [52] In a moment, in the twinkling of an eye, at the last trump: for the trumpet shall sound and the dead shall be raised incorruptible, and we shall be changed. [53] For this corruptible must put on incorruption, and this mortal must put on immortality. [54] So when this corruptible shall have put on incorruption, and this mortal shall have put on immortality, then shall be brought to pass the saying that is written, Death is swallowed up in victory. [55] O death, where is thy sting? O grave, where is thy victory? [56] The sting of death is sin; and the strength of sin is the law.**

During the ministry I have encountered many questions about what the new body will be like. I don't think it is possible to know everything about our future body. The Bible does give us a lot of information about our future body.

21

Let us learn from the scriptures what our new glorified body will be like.

I.   Our new glorified body will be like the body of Christ.

Philippians 3:21 Who shall change our vile body, that it may be fashioned like unto his glorious body, according to the working whereby he is able even to subdue all things unto himself.

I John 3:2 Beloved, now are we the sons of God, and it doth not yet appear what we shall be: but we know that, when he shall appear, we shall be like him; for we shall see him as he is.

   A.   We learn from these passages that our new body will be like the body that Jesus had after the resurrection. Knowing this, we can study the body of our resurrected Savior and also be studying what our future body will be like.

   B.   Right now, we are Christians, which means Christ like. Our capabilities now are limited because of our body or our flesh. Thank God, this problem will be forever solved when we are given our glorified body like the one Jesus has.

C.   I can think of no other person in history whose body I would want to be patterned after. With this fact in mind, let us proceed further to learn about our future body.

II. Our new glorified body will be a body of flesh and bone.

St. Luke 24:39 Behold my hands and my feet, that it is I myself: handle me, and see; for a spirit hath no flesh and bones, as ye see me have.

A.   This body will have substance. Jesus could be touched and handled. There is a skeletal system which gives height and depth to this body.

B.   This body also has flesh which gives the body its appearance. Even before these scriptures Job knew this.

Job 19:25-26 For I know that my redeemer liveth, and that he shall stand at the latter day upon the earth: [26] And though after my skin worms destroy this body, yet in my flesh shall I see God:

III. Our new glorified body will be recognizable.

I Corinthians 13:12 For now we see through a glass, darkly; but then

face to face: now I know in part; but then shall I know even as also I am known.

A. Some feel that we will all look like Jesus. I do not. We will not be clones. We will be able to recognize each other in Heaven.

B. Each of us now has our own distinct characteristics. When we get our new glorified body, we will still have our own distinct characteristics.

I Corinthians 15:41-44 There is one glory of the sun, and another glory of the moon, and another glory of the stars: for one star differeth from another star in glory. [42] So also is the resurrection of the dead.   It is sown in corruption; it is raised in incorruption: [43] It is sown in dishonour; it is raised in glory: it is sown in weakness; it is raised in power: [44] It is sown a natural body; it is raised a spiritual body. There is a natural body, and there is a spiritual body.

Just as each star is different from another, so, also, will be our new glorified body.   The new knowledge that we will have in these bodies will enable us to know everyone. I believe that we will know Paul, Stephen, Timothy, John and all the others without having to be introduced.

IV. Our new glorified body will be a body in which the spirit dominates.

I Corinthians 15:44 It is sown a natural body; it is raised a spiritual body. There is a natural body, and there is a spiritual body.

A. Right now we are in a body that the flesh most commonly dominates. Sometimes our greatest battle is with the desires of the flesh.

James 1:13-14 Let no man say when he is tempted, I am tempted of God: for God cannot be tempted with evil, neither tempteth he any man: [14] But every man is tempted, when he is drawn away of his own lust, and enticed.

B. Right now the spirit usually submits to the flesh. This does not always have to be the case, even now. It takes a strong spiritual person to win over the flesh. Even though we may defeat the flesh, it is a constant battle.

Mark 14:38 Watch ye and pray, lest ye enter into temptation.

The spirit truly is ready, but the flesh is weak.

Praise the Lord, this battle will soon be over. Our new body will have such a strong spirit that the flesh will always submit to the spirit.

V. Our new glorified body will be unlimited by time, space or even gravity. Remember that our new body will be like the resurrected body of our Savior.

    A. Jesus was able to appear and vanish right before their eyes.

        St. Luke 24:31-36 And their eyes were opened, and they knew him; and he vanished out of their sight. [32] And they said one to another, Did not our heart burn within us, while he talked with us by the way, and while he opened to us the scriptures? [33] And they rose up the same hour, and returned to Jerusalem, and found the eleven gathered together, and them that were with them, [34] Saying, The Lord is risen indeed, and hath appeared to Simon. [35] And they told what things were done in the way, and how he was known of them in breaking of bread. [36] And as they thus spake, Jesus himself stood in the midst of them, and

saith unto them, Peace be unto you.

B.   This also happened even in the midst of secured rooms.

St. John 20:19   Then the same day at evening, being the first day of the week, when the doors were shut where the disciples were assembled for fear of the jews, came Jesus and stood in the midst, and saith unto them, Peace be unto you.

St. John 20:26 ... Thomas with them: then came Jesus, the doors being shut, and stood in the midst, and said, peace be unto you.

C.   I personally believe that because this body is spirit controlled, the body will be able to travel by the will of the spirit.   Right now our spirit is within our flesh, and the flesh transports or carries the spirit from place to place. In our new glorified body the spirit will transport the flesh.   This will not be with wings. We will not have wings. I personally believe that this transportation will be by thought, through the will of the spirit.   In other words, you will just have to think that you want to be at a certain place and you will be

27

there. Glory to God, this will be better than any transportation available to us now.

VI. Our new glorified body will be an eternal body.

II Corinthians 5:1 For we know that if our earthly house of this tabernacle were dissolved, we have a building of God, an house not made with hands, eternal in the heavens.

A. This new body will never, never, never wear out. The aging process will not affect this new body.

Today our society spends billions of dollars each year to feel better and look younger. Praise God, this will not be necessary in our new glorified body.

B. This new glorified body will be youthful, able and energetic forever. This new glorified body will be more fit than any olympian. It will never be out of shape, never underweight or overweight. What an exciting thought!

VII. Our new glorified body will be a glorious body.

I Corinthians 15:43 It is sown in dishonour, it is raised in glory:

it is sown in weakness; it is raised in power.

Romans 8:18 For I reckon that the sufferings of the present time are not worthy to be compared with the glory which shall be revealed in us.

A.   We have been calling this our new glorified body. What does it mean to be glorified. A study of this word reveals quite a lot. Not only does glorified mean beautiful but much more. Studying the Greek of this word suggests that this body will be bright even to the point of shining.

Daniel 12:3 And they that be wise shall shine as the brightness of the firmament; and they that turn many to righteousness as the stars for ever and ever.

B.   The new body will not be troubled with the things that this body is troubled with. There will be no blindness and no aches or pains. There will be no colds or cancer. There will be no problems such as being deaf or dumb, having heart problems, or tumors. Truly this is a glorified body. Sometimes I can't wait to get into my new glorified body and use it to praise the one who made it possible.Christians

will be given the body at the
Rapture of the church. We will
have this body from that time
on forever. As we study
prophecy from this point
forward, Christians do have
their new glorified bodies.

THE JUDGMENT SEAT OF CHRIST

I. What is the Judgment Seat of Christ?

II. Who will be involved in the Judgment Seat of Christ?

III. What will the Lord Jesus Christ be concerned with at the Judgment Seat of Christ?

IV. What will be the results of the Judgment Seat of Christ?

As we begin this lesson on The
Judgment Seat of Christ, let us be aware
that there is more than one judgment
taught in the scriptures.   Too many
times, even Christians believe that there
will be one judgment at the end of time.
This is not the case; however, we hope to
give you a clear picture of one of the
judgments in this lesson called The
Judgment Seat of Christ.

I.   What   is   the   Judgment   Seat   of
      Christ?

      A.   The Judgment Seat of Christ is
            where all believers will stand
            and give an account for their
            stewardship. There are several
            verses of scripture that teach
            us this.

            **Romans 14:10-12   But why dost
            thou judge thy brother? or Why
            dost thou set at nought thy
            brother?   For   we   shall   all
            stand before the judgment seat
            of Christ.   [11] For it is
            written, As I live, saith the
            Lord, every knee shall bow to
            me, and every tongue shall
            confess to God.   [12] So then
            everyone of us shall give
            account of himself to God.**

            **I   Corinthians   3:11-15   For
            other foundation can no man lay
            than   that   is   laid,   which   is
            Jesus Christ.   [12] Now if any
            man build upon this foundation
            gold, silver, precious stone,**

wood, hay, stubble; [13] Every man's work shall be made manifest: for the day shall declare it, because it shall be revealed by fire; and the fire shall try every man's work of what sort it is. [14] If any man's work abide which he hath built thereupon, he shall receive a reward. [15] If any man's work shall be burned, he shall suffer loss: but he himself shall be saved; yet so as by fire.

II Corinthians 5:10 For we must all appear before the judgment seat of Christ; That every one may receive the things done in his body, according to that he hath done, whether it be good or bad.

Keep in mind that Paul is talking to his brothers in the Lord, and includes himself when he uses the word we.

B.   The Judgment Seat of Christ is concerned with giving rewards. The words Judgment Seat comes from a greek word Bema which was commonly used during that time. Historians tell us that there was a raised platform in the arenas where the athletes stood to receive their rewards. This raised platform where the judge sat was a place of dignity and honor, and it was where the judge gave out the rewards. This is why the Judgment Seat of Christ is also sometimes called the Bema Judgment.

II. Who will be involved in the Judgment Seat of Christ?

A. Of course, there is the Judge, and it is called the Judgment Seat of Christ. So the Judge is none other than the Lord Jesus Christ.

St. John 5:22 For the Father judgeth no man, but hath committed all judgment to the Son:

Truly we can rejoice in the fact that the Judgment Seat of Christ will have the most knowledgeable, righteous Judge that could ever be. A Judge that knows what we have to deal with every day of our lives.

Hebrews 4:15 For we have not a high priest which cannot be touched with the feeling of our infirmities; but was in all points tempted like as we are, yet without sin.

B. The others who will be involved in the Judgment Seat of Christ are all the raptured believers. There will be no unsaved people at this judgment. In the three passages of scripture that we used at the beginning of this lesson, Paul used the word "we" indicating his fellow Christians and himself. The Judge will be the Lord Jesus Christ, and all the believers will stand before him at the judgment seat of Christ.

III. What will the Lord Jesus Christ be concerned with at this judgment?

A.   It is important that we realize that Jesus will not be concerned with punishing believers for sin. When we accepted Jesus as Savior, the sin problem was dealt with then.

I John 1:7 But if we walk in the light, as he is in the light, we have fellowship one with another, and the blood of Jesus Christ his Son cleanseth us from all sin.

This cleansing from all sin took place when we got saved, and God has promised that he would not remember our sin.

Hebrews 8:12 For I will be merciful to their unrighteousness, and their sins and their iniquities will I remember no more.

Hebrews 10:17   And their sins and iniquities will I remember no more.

Psalm 103:12   As far as the east is from the west, so far hath   he   removed   our transgressions from us.

Praise   the   Lord   for   the forgiveness   of   sin!   This judgment   will   not   be   to determine who goes to Heaven or hell.   The question of Heaven or hell is determined here on earth   while   each   person   is alive.

St.   John   3:18   He   that believeth   on   him   is   not condemned: but   he   that believeth   not   is   condemned already,because   he   hath   not believed   in   the   name   of   the only begotten Son of God.

B.   Jesus   will   be   concerned with how Christians have conducted themselves   concerning   their stewardship.

I Peter 4:10 As every man hath received   the   gift,   even   so minister   the   same   one   to another,   as   good   stewards   of the manifold grace of God.

I Corinthians 4:1-2 Let a man so   account   of   us,   as   of   the ministers   of   Christ,   and

36

**stewards of the mysteries of
God. Moreover, it is required
in stewards, that a man be
found faithful.**

At this point we need to learn
more about what a steward is.
A steward was a person that was
in charge of a large household
or estate. He was to keep
things going in a manner that
would please the only one that
he was to answer to which was
the owner. With this in mind,
we can realize that we will be
judged on how faithful we have
been in our Christian life.
And how we have managed
ourselves and our privileges
and responsibilities since we
became Christians.

C. While the stewardship summary
    gives us the examples of how we
    will be dealt with, we also
    need to be aware of some
    specifics with which Jesus will
    be concerned.

One thing that we really need
to remember is that Jesus will
be concerned with the reasons
we did the works we did. In
other words what was our motive
for doing what we did? There
are many good works that will
go up in smoke because they
were done for ungodly, selfish
reasons.

I Corinthians 3:13 Every man's work shall be made manifest:

II Corinthians 5:11 ... but we are made manifest unto God;

Notice the use of the word manifest in these verses, it means to be opened up or brought to the light.

I Corinthians 4:5 Therefore judge nothing before the time until the Lord come, who both will bring to light the hidden things of darkness, and will make manifest the counsels of the hearts; and then shall every man have praise of God.

Notice the phrase manifest the counsels of the hearts, this means that the thoughts and motives of each Christian will be revealed.

Another area we need to think about is all of those things we should be doing for the Lord that we do not get done.

James 4:17 Therefore to him that knoweth to do good, and doeth it not, to him it is sin.

Let us not procrastinate doing those things we feel the Lord wants us to do.

The last area we will mention here is the area of works that we do. We will cover this also in the section on the results of the Judgment Seat of Christ. Let us state here that why we do the works is just as important as the works that we do. All of our works will be tested.

I Corinthians 3:13 Every man's work shall be made manifest: for the day shall declare it, because it shall be revealed by fire; and the fire shall try every man's work of what sort it is.

We will begin to notice what some of the works are that bring rewards in the next section.

IV. What are the results of the Judgement Seat of Christ?

    A. Some will suffer loss. They will lose their reward in part, because the motive for the works they were doing were wrong.

    I Corinthians 3:15 If any man's work shall be burned, he shall suffer loss: but he himself shall be saved; yet so as by fire.

The Christian that does good works that would be rewarded but turns to carnality may very well lose those rewards.

II John 1:8 Look to yourselves, that we lose not those things which we have wrought, but that we receive a full reward.

B. Not all will suffer loss, others will receive rewards for the good works they have done.

I Corinthians 1:14 If any man's work abide which he hath built thereupon, he shall receive a reward.

In the Bible we find that there are at least five rewards mentioned for those who will be receiving them. The incorruptible crown will be given to those who overcome the selfish and sinful desires of the old nature.

I Corinthians 9:25-27 And every man that striveth for the mastery is temperate in all things. Now they do it to obtain a corruptible crown; but we an incorruptible. [26] I therefore so run, not as uncertainly; so flight I, not as one that beateth the air: [27] But I keep under my body, and bring it into subjection:

least that by any means, when I have preached to others, I myself should be a castaway.

The crown of rejoicing will be given to those who witness to and lead souls to the Lord.

I Thessalonians 2:19—20   For what is our hope, or joy, or crown of rejoicing?   Are not even ye in the presence of our Lord Jesus Christ at his coming?   [20] For ye are our glory and joy.

The crown of life will be given to those who overcome in times of trials, sufferings and temptations.

Revelation 2:10   Fear none of those things which thou shalt suffer: behold, the devil shall cast some of you in prison that ye may be tried; and ye shall have tribulation ten days: be thou faithful unto death, and I will give thee a crown of life.

The crown of righteousness will be given to those who especially long for and look for the day when Jesus will come for his Saints.

II Timothy 4:8   Henceforth there is laid up for me a crown of righteousness, which the

41

Lord, the righteous judge, shall give me at that day: and not to me only, but unto all them also that love his appearing.

The crown of glory will be given to faithful preachers and teachers who feed the people of God.

I Peter 5:2-4 Feed the flock of God which is among you, taking the oversight thereof, not by constraint, but willingly; not for filthy lucre, but of a ready mind; [3] Neither as being Lords over God's heritage, but being examples to the flock. [4] And when the chief Shepherd shall appear, ye shall receive a crown of glory that fadeth not away.

Whatever these crowns are or whatever they represent, they will be used to glorify the Lord.

Revelation 4:10 The four and twenty elders fall down before him that sat on the throne, and worship him that liveth for ever and ever, and cast their crowns before the throne, saying,

What else would we want to do with our crowns but use them to praise the one who died for our sins?

C.   There should also be some results of the Judgment Seat of Christ present right now in our lives. Knowing that we will stand before the Lord Jesus Christ and give an account of our deeds done in this body as Christians should help us want to live our lives to please the Lord.

I John 2:28 And now, little children, abide in him; that, when he shall appear, we may have confidence, and not be ashamed before him at his coming.

One of the reasons the Corinthian church was having so many problems, was because they were forgetting future judgment. Let us avoid many problems in our Christian lives, and let us have a closer relationship with the Lord by remembering that some day we will stand before the Judgment Seat of Christ.

THE MARRIAGE AND SUPPER OF THE LAMB

I. The proof of the marriage.

II. The place of the marriage.

III. The participants of the marriage.

IV. The pattern of the marriage.

Now that we have a better understanding of the Rapture and the Judgment Seat of Christ, let us turn our attention to the Marriage and Supper of the Lamb.

Weddings usually bring a touch of excitement to all involved. This is the wedding of all weddings, so let us approach this subject with a lot of excitement. In this wedding, no expense will be spared for the father of the groom owns it all. No pre-nuptial agreement will be needed for this marriage will last forever. No cold feet will be experienced because this is the most desired marriage of the ages.

Let us now walk down the aisle of the scriptures and view this wedding through the pages of God's word.

I.   The proof of the marriage.

Throughout this lesson we will be using many passages of scripture which speak of the marriage. So we are going to list just a few here to show that the greatest wedding in the universe has yet to take place.

Romans 7:4 Wherefore, my brethren, ye also are become dead to the law by the body of Christ; that ye should be married to another, even to him who is raised from the dead, that we should bring forth fruit unto God.

II Corinthians 11:2 For I am jealous over you with godly jealousy: for I have espoused you to one husband, that I may present you as a chaste virgin to Christ.

Revelation 19:7-9 Let us be glad and rejoice, and give honour to him: for the marriage of the Lamb is come, and his wife hath made herself ready. [8] And to her was granted that she should be arrayed in fine linen, clean and white: for the fine linen is the righteousness of saints. [9] And he saith unto me, Write, Blessed are they which are called unto the marriage supper of the Lamb. And he saith unto me, These are the true sayings of God.

This is, no doubt, a great subject with many passages from the Word of God.

II. The place of the marriage.

    A. First let us notice the marriage place in time.

        1. We know that the marriage will take place before The second coming of Christ to the earth, and it seems to follow shortly after The Judgement Seat of Christ we just studied.

        2. With this in mind we can see the events as

follows: The Rapture, The Judgment Seat of Christ, then The Marriage of the Lamb followed by The Second Coming of Christ to this earth.

B. Second, let us notice where the wedding will take place. Since the marriage follows immediately after The Judgment Seat of Christ, it will certainly take place in Heaven. It is from Heaven that the church will return with Christ just after the wedding.

Revelation 19:11 & 14   And I saw heaven opened, and behold a white horse, and he that sat upon him was called Faithful and True, and in righteousness he doth judge and make war. ... [14] And the armies which were in heaven followed him upon white horses, clothed in fine linen, white and clean.

Praise God this wedding of weddings will take place in the place of all places. What a beautiful scene as the bride and groom get married in Heaven.

III. The participants of the marriage.

A. No doubt God the Father will be involved in the marriage. He is pictured as the host,

preparing and sending servants
out to invite the guests.

**St. Luke 14:16—23   [16] Then
said he unto him, A certain man
made a great supper, and bade
many; [17] And sent his servant
at supper time to say to them
that were bidden.   Come; for
all things are now ready. [18]
And they all with one consent
began to make excuse.   The
first said unto him, I have
bought a piece of ground, and I
must needs go and see it: I
pray thee have me excused.
[19] And another said, I have
bought five yoke of oxen, and I
go to prove them: I pray thee
have me excused.   [20] And
another said, I have married a
wife, and therefore I cannot
come.   [21] So that servant
came and shewed his lord these
things. Then the master of the
house being angry said to his
servant, Go out quickly into
the streets and lanes of the
city, and bring in hither the
poor, and the maimed, and the
halt, and the blind. [22] And
the servant said, Lord, it is
done as thou hast commanded,
and yet there is room.   [23]
And the lord said unto the
servant, Go out into the
highways and hedges and compel
them to come in, that my house
may be filled.**

B. Then the bridegroom is none other than the Lord Jesus Christ. John the Baptist points this out.

St. John 3:27-30 John answered and said, A man can receive nothing, except it be given him from heaven. [28] Ye yourselves bear me witness, that I said, I am not the Christ, but that I am sent before him. [29] He that hath the bride is the bridegroom: but the friend of the bridegroom, which standeth and heareth him, rejoiceth greatly because of the bridegroom's voice: this my joy therefore is fulfilled. [30] He must increase, but I must decrease.

And Jesus also calls himself the bridegroom.

St. Luke 5:32-35 I came not to call the righteous, but sinners to repentance. [33] And they said unto him, Why do the disciples of John fast often, and make prayers, and likewise the disciples of the Pharisees; but thine eat and drink? [34] And he said unto them, Can ye make the children of the bride chamber fast, while the bridegroom is with them? [35] But the days will come, when the bridegroom shall be taken

away from them, and then shall they fast in those days.

Truly this bridegroom is the fairest of all, the rose of Sharon, the lily of the valley, the bravest and most honorable groom to ever take a wife.

C. The third participant is the bride. We can't have a wedding without a bride and what a bride she is. Two passages of scripture distinctly identify the bride as the church.

Ephesians 5:22-32 Wives, submit yourselves unto your own husbands, as unto the Lord. [23] For the husband is the head of the wife, even as Christ is the head of the church; and he is the Savior of the body. [24] Therefore as the church is subject unto Christ, so let the wives be to their own husbands in every thing. [25] Husbands, love your wives, even as Christ also loved the church, and gave himself for it. [26] That he might sanctify and cleanse it with the washing of water by the word. [27] That he might present it to himself a glorious church not having spot, or wrinkle, or any such thing, but that it should be holy and without blemish. [28] So ought men to love their wives as their own bodies. He that loveth his wife loveth himself. [29] For no man ever yet hated his own flesh; but nourisheth and cherisheth it, even as the Lord the church. [30] For we are members of his body, of his flesh, and of his bones. [31] For this cause shall a man leave his father and mother, and shall be joined unto his wife, and they two shall be one flesh. [32] This is a great mystery: but I speak concerning Christ and the church.

II Corinthians 11:2 For I am jealous over you with godly jealousy; for I have espoused you to one husband, that I may present you as a chaste virgin to Christ.

Every man, woman, boy and girl that has accepted Jesus since the day of pentecost until the day of the Rapture, [a time period called the church age] will be a part of the bride.

D. We have the Father as the host. The Son as the groom and the Church as the bride. Then we have a fourth group of people who we are going to call the invited guests.

Revelation 19:9 And he saith unto me, Write, Blessed are

51

they which are called unto the marriage supper of the Lamb. And he saith unto me, These are the true sayings of God.

They are called or invited to the ceremony, and I believe that they are friends of the bridegroom.

St. John 3:29 He that hath the bride is the bridegroom; but the friend of the bridegroom, which standeth and heareth him, rejoiceth greatly because of the bridegroom's voice; this my joy therefore is fulfilled.

There is much debate over who is included in this group. But most all agree that those who were believers before pentecost make up this group. This would include all the Old Testament Saints.

IV.   The pattern of The Marriage of the Lamb.

The pattern of The Marriage will follow the original pattern of marriage that we find in the New Testament. This Marriage consisted of three separate stages called the betrothal, presentation and celebration stages.

A. The betrothal stage.

It was during this time that the grooms father would promise his son to a chosen girl. This would happen while the couple were children. The father would then make a proper down payment and sign the legal papers. In many cases the bride and groom had never seen each other, yet they were betrothed. Mary and Joseph are examples of this.

St. Matthew 1:18 Now the birth of Jesus Christ was on this wise: When as his mother Mary was espoused to Joseph, before they came together, she was found with child of the Holy Ghost.

So we see that the betrothal stage had two parts: (1) The selection of the bride. (2) The payment of the dowry. With this in mind we can realize the bride has been selected.

Ephesians 1:3-4 Blessed be the God and Father of our Lord Jesus Christ who hath blessed us with all spiritual blessings in heavenly places in Christ. [4] According as he hath chosen us in him before the foundation of the world, that we should be holy and without blame before him in love.

And the highest of all dowry's has been paid. The dowry being the precious blood of Jesus.

I Corinthians 6:19-20   What? Know ye not that your body is the temple of the Holy Ghost which is in you, which ye have of God, and ye are not your own?   [20] For ye are bought with a price: therefore glorify God in your body, and in your spirit, which are God's.

I Peter 1:18-19   Forasmuch as ye know that ye were not redeemed with corruptible things, as silver and gold, from your vain conversation received by tradition from your fathers; [19] But with the precious blood of Christ, as of a lamb without blemish and without spot.

This takes us to the second stage.

B.   The presentation stage.

It was during this time that the father would send for the bride.   The bride would be brought to the father's house, and at the proper time, the father would present the bride to the groom by placing their hands together.

No doubt this second stage has yet to take place. But it will soon start in the Rapture of the Church as the Father calls for the Bride.

Revelation 4:1 After this I looked, and behold; a door was opened in heaven; and the first voice which I heard was as it were of a trumpet talking with me; which said, Come up hither, and I will show thee things which must be hereafter.

He brings the bride to his house.

St. John 14:23 Jesus answered and said unto him, If a man love me, he will keep my words; and my Father will love him, and we will come unto him, and make our abode with him.

Jude 24 Now unto him that is able to keep you from falling, and to present you faultless before the presence of his glory with exceeding joy.

Praise God, I hope that reading this has excited you as much as writing it has excited me. Truly this brings us to the celebration stage.

C.   The celebration stage.

After the wedding, they would have a public marriage supper. It was during such a time that Jesus performed his first miracle as recorded in St. John 2.

What a time of celebration as the bride and groom have come together in one of the greatest events of all time.

Revelation 19:9 And he saith unto me. Write, Blessed are they which are called unto the marriage supper of the Lamb. And he saith unto me. These are the true sayings of God.

And what a supper it will be as the Lord girds himself and serves.

St. Luke 12:35-37 Let your loins be girded about, and your lights burning. [36] And ye yourselves like unto men that wait for their lord, when he will return from the wedding; that when he cometh and knocketh, they may open unto him immediately. [37] Blessed are those servants, whom the Lord when he cometh shall find watching; verily I say unto you that he shall gird himself, and make them to sit down to meat, and will come forth and serve them.

There is no way to sum up this lesson. However, I believe that leaving you with the Psalm of the wedding of the King would be appropriate.

Psalm 45 My heart is inditing a good matter: I speak of the things which I have made touching the king: my tongue is the pen of a ready writer. [2] Thou art fairer than the children of men: grace is poured into thy lips: therefore God hath blessed thee for ever. [3] Gird thy sword upon thy thigh, O most mighty, with thy glory and thy majesty. [4] And in thy majesty ride prosperously because of truth and meekness and righteousness; and thy right hand shall teach thee terrible things. [5] Thine arrows are sharp in the heart of the king's enemies; whereby the people fall under thee. [6] Thy throne, O God, is for ever and ever: the sceptre of thy kingdom is a right sceptre. [7] Thou lovest righteousness, and hatest wickedness: therefore God, thy God, hath anointed thee with the oil of gladness above thy fellows. [8] All thy garments smell of myrrh, and aloes, and cassia, out of the ivory palaces, whereby they have made thee glad. [9] Kings' daughters were among thy

honourable women: upon thy right hand did stand the queen in gold of Ophir. [10] Hearken, O daughter, and consider, and incline thine ear; forget also thine own people, and thy father's house; [11] So shall the king greatly desire thy beauty: for he is thy Lord; and worship thou him. [12] And the daughter of Tyre shall be there with a gift; even the rich among the people shall intreat thy favour. [13] The king's daughter is all glorious within: her clothing is of wrought gold. [14] She shall be brought unto the king in raiment of needlework: the virgins her companions that follow her shall be brought unto thee. [15] With gladness and rejoicing shall they be brought: they shall enter into the king's palace. [16] Instead of thy fathers shall be thy children, whom thou mayest make princes in all the earth. [17] I will make thy name to be remembered in all generations: therefore shall the people praise thee for ever and ever.

THE TRIBULATION

I.   The titles of the Tribulation.

II. The purpose of the Tribulation.

III. The mark of the Tribulation.

IV. The 144,000 of the Tribulation.

V.   The two witnesses of the Tribulation.

VI. The action of the Tribulation.

Our goal in this lesson is simply to give an overview of a period of time most commonly called the Tribulation. If we were to make an extensive study on this subject, we would be studying it for a long time. This lesson would be longer than all of the others combined. We encourage you to study this subject further using this lesson to get you started.

Now, let us dive into a time and place called the Tribulation. I pray that you will only study about the Tribulation and will never experience the Tribulation. All of the saved will leave this earth in The Rapture and will be at The Marriage and Supper of The Lamb while The Tribulation is happening on earth.

I.   The titles for the period.

If anyone were going to make a study on the period, it would be necessary to know the titles that are used in the Bible to refer to The Tribulation.

A.   The Day of the Lord.

This is the most common name for this period and is found throughout the Old and New Testaments. Some examples are: **Isaiah 2:12   Isaiah 13:6, 9 Ezekiel 13:5   Joel 1:15 I Thessalonians 5:2   II Peter 3:10** There are also several others.

B. The Day of God's Vengeance
    Isaiah 34:8   Isaiah 63:1-6

C. The Time of Jacob's Trouble
    Jeremiah 30:7

D. The Seventieth Week
    Daniel 9:24-27

E. The Time of the End
    Daniel 12:9

F. The Great Day of his Wrath
    Revelation 6:17

G. The Hour of His Judgment
    Revelation 14:7

H. The End of the World
    Matthew 13:40, 49

I. The Indignation
    Isaiah 26:20   Isaiah 34:2

J. The Overspread of Abominations
    Daniel 9:27

K. Day of Trouble
    Daniel 12:1   Zephaniah 1:14,15

L. The Tribulation
    Matthew 24:21, 29

Knowing these titles will help you
in your personal study of this
period. We will use the last title
for reference to this time.
Throughout the remainder of this
lesson, we will call this period the
tribulation period.

61

Now that we know the titles of this period, let us move on to the purpose of The Tribulation.

II. The purpose of The Tribulation.

Throughout my ministry I have been asked many times, "What is the reason or purpose of The Tribulation?"

A. To prepare Israel for her Messiah.

This is the primary purpose of The Tribulation.

Ezekiel 20:37-38 And I will cause you to pass under the rod, and I will bring you into the bond of the covenant: [38] And I will purge out from among you the rebels, and them that transgress against me: I will bring them forth out of the country where they sojourn, and they shall not enter into the land of Israel: and ye shall know that I am the Lord. Zechariah 13:8-9 And it shall come to pass, that in all the land, saith the Lord, two parts therein shall be cut off and die; but the third shall be left therein. And I will bring the third part through the fire, and will refine them as silver is refined, and will try them as gold is tried: they shall call on my name, and I

will hear them: I will say, It is my people: and they shall say, The Lord is my God.

Malachi 3:3 And he shall sit as a refiner and purifier of silver: and he shall purify the sons of Levi, and purge them as gold and silver, that they may offer unto the Lord an offering in righteousness.

There is no doubt that The Tribulation will affect everyone on the earth as it unfolds. It is called the seventieth week. This is a seven year time period that God promises to deal primarily with the Jews.

B.   To pour out judgment on the unrighteousness.

Romans 1:18 For the wrath of God is revealed from heaven against all ungodliness and unrighteousness of men, who hold the truth in unrighteousness;

II Thessalonians 2:11-12 And for this cause God shall send them strong delusion, that they should believe a lie: [12] That they all might be damned who believed not the truth, but had pleasure in unrighteousness.

63

Isaiah 26:21 For, behold, the Lord cometh out of his place to punish the inhabitants of the earth for their iniquity: the earth also shall disclose her blood, and shall no more cover her slain.

This is necessary to bring about a time when the earth will be filled with the knowledge of God.

III. The mark of the Tribulation.

Revelation 13:16-18 And he causeth all, both small and great, rich and poor, free and bond, to receive a mark in their right hand, or in their foreheads: [17] And that no man might buy or sell, save he that had the mark, or the name of the beast, or the number of his name. [18] Here is wisdom. Let him that hath understanding count the number of the beast: for it is the number of a man; and his number is six hundred threescore and six.

Many have made attempts to identify the antichrist using the mark 666. My personal opinion is that this antichrist will not be recognized until after The Tribulation has started. There are several facts that we do know about this mark, let us take time to examine them.

A. The mark is the number of man. Numbers in the Bible have meaning. For example, the number seven is the number of perfection. The number six is the number of man. It is one short of being complete. This antichrist is still on the level of man.

B. The mark will be necessary to trade.

Revelation 13:17 And that no man might buy or sell, save he that had the mark, or the name of the beast, or the number of his name.

To get food, clothing or any other things necessary to live during the Tribulation, one will have to have this mark.

The required mark will have to be in the right hand or in the forehead. It may be visible to the natural eye, or the mark may be ultraviolet. But the mark will be required to work, sell or make any purchases.

C. The mark invokes God's wrath.

Revelation 16:2 And the first went, and poured out his vial upon the earth; and there fell a noisome and grievous sore upon the men which had the mark

of the beast, and upon them which worshipped his image.

A terrible sore will come specifically for those who have the mark.

D.   The mark will seal ones future.

Revelation 14:9-11   And the third angel followed them, saying with a loud voice, If any man worship the beast and his image, and receive his mark in his forehead, or in his hand, [10] The same shall drink of the wine of the wrath of God, which is poured out without mixture into the cup of his indignation; and he shall be tormented with fire and brimstone in the presence of the holy angels, and in the presence of the Lamb: [11] And the smoke of their torment ascendeth up for ever and ever: and they have no rest day nor night, who worship the beast and his image, and whosoever receiveth the mark of his name.

Revelation 19:20 And the beast was taken, and with him the false prophet that wrought miracles before him, with which he deceived them that had received the mark of the beast, and them that worshipped his image.   These both were cast

alive into a lake of fire burning with brimstone.

The mark is like signing a contract with the devil. When a person receives the mark, his future destination is the lake of fire. There is no way to change this.

IV.   The 144,000 of the Tribulation.

Revelation 7:2-4 And I saw another angel ascending from the east, having the seal of the living God: and he cried with a loud voice to the four angels, to whom it was given to hurt the earth and the sea, [3] Saying, Hurt not the earth, neither the sea, nor the trees, till we have sealed the servants of our God in their foreheads. [4] And I heard the number of them which were sealed: and there were sealed an hundred and forty and four thousand of all the tribes of the children of Israel.

There has been a lot of speculation about who these people are and what they represent. Some believe that only these 144,000 will not receive the mark of the beast and come through The Tribulation. Others believe that only 144,000 will get to go to Heaven. As we approach this subject, let us rightly divide the Word of God so that we may understand this.

A.   They are 12,000 from each tribe.

Revelation 7:5-8 Of the tribe of Juda were sealed twelve thousand. Of the tribe of Reuben were sealed twelve thousand. Of the tribe of Gad were sealed twelve thousand. [6] Of the tribe of Aser were sealed twelve thousand. Of the tribe of Nepthalim were sealed twelve thousand. Of the tribe of Manasses were sealed twelve thousand. [7] Of the tribe of Simeon were sealed twelve thousand. Of the tribe of Levi were sealed twelve thousand. Of the tribe of Issachar were sealed twelve thousand. [8] Of the tribe of Zabulon were sealed twelve thousand. Of the tribe of Joseph were sealed twelve thousand. Of the tribe of Benjamin were sealed twelve thousand.

Truly there would be difficulty on the part of man to identify twelve thousand from each tribe of Israel. There will be no difficulty on the part of God. God still knows the tribe from which every one descended. There will be 12,000 from twelve tribes making up the 144,000.

B.   They are servants of God.

Revelation 7:3   Saying, Hurt not the earth, neither the sea, nor the trees, till we have sealed the servants of our God in their foreheads.

These men are special servants of the Lord during The Tribulation. They are actually sealed with the seal of God in their foreheads. My opinion is that this happens before the mark of the beast is invoked, just after The Rapture of the church. The mark of the beast (666) is Satan's attempt to copy God. Satan is a copier and not a creator.

Revelation 14:4   These are they which were not defiled with women; for they are virgins. These are they which follow the Lamb whithersoever he goeth. These were redeemed from among men, being the firstfruits unto God and to the Lamb.

These special servants are totally committed to God. They are not married. Their only commitment is to do the work of God.

C.   They have a special message.

St. Matthew 24:14   And this gospel of the kingdom shall be

preached in all the world for a witness unto all nations; and then shall the end come.

Matthew, Chapter 24, is a tribulation chapter. This verse teaches that the gospel of the kingdom will have to be preached in all the world, and then the end will come. We are today preaching the gospel of grace. This message will end at The Rapture of the Church. The new message will be the gospel of the Kingdom, and you have to endure until the end to get into the kingdom that Jesus is coming to set up.

The 144,000 servants of God will take this message to the whole world before the end.

I am not waiting for the gospel to be preached in all the world before The Rapture. This will happen during The Tribulation by the 144,000.

D.   They have a special place.

Revelation 14:3 And they sung as it were a new song before the throne, and before the four beasts and the elders: and no man could learn that song but the hundred and forty and four thousand, which were redeemed from the earth.

I believe this is a special
song of victory because their
ministry was effective. A
great multitude of all people
will come out of The
Tribulation because of the
ministry of the 144,000.

**Revelation 7:9 After this I
beheld, and, lo, a great
multitude, which no man could
number, of all nations, and
kindreds, and people, and
tongues, stood before the
throne, and before the Lamb,
clothed with white robes, and
palms in their hands;**

**Revelation 7:13-14 And one of
the elders answered, saying
unto me, What are these which
are arrayed in white robes?
and Whence came they? [14] And
I said unto him, Sir, thou
knowest. And he said to me,
These are they which came out
of great tribulation, and have
washed their robes, and made
them white in the blood of the
Lamb.**

There will be mostly Jews that
come through The Tribulation.
However, because of the 144,000
there will be people of all
nations.

V. The two witnesses of the
Tribulation.

Revelation 11:3 And I will give power unto my two witnesses, and they shall prophesy a thousand two hundred and threescore days, clothed in sackcloth.

There are a lot of questions about who these two men are. Most theologians believe that these men will be either Elijah and Moses, or Elijah and Enoch. While it is hard to be sure of who they are, we can be sure of what happens to them.

A.   These two have special power.

Revelation 11:5 And if any man will hurt them, fire proceedeth out of their mouth, and devoureth their enemies: and if any man will hurt them, he must in this manner be killed.

Revelation 11:6 These have power to shut heaven, that it rain not in the days of their prophecy: and have power over waters to turn them to blood, and to smite the earth with all plagues, as often as they will.

Fire will come from them to protect them until their work is done. They will have power to cause it not to rain for three and a half years. They will have power to turn the waters to blood and to smite the earth with plagues. These two witnesses are the light of

God to the world during this part of The Tribulation.

Revelation 11:4 These are the two olive trees, and the two candlesticks standing before the God of the earth.

B.   These two have limited time.

Revelation 11:3 And I will give power unto my two witnesses, and they shall prophesy a thousand two hundred and threescore days, clothed in sackcloth.

Revelation 11:7 And when they shall have finished their testimony, the beast that ascendeth out of the bottomless pit shall make war against them, and shall overcome them, and kill them.

They cannot be killed until their work is done. They will be killed by the beast.

C.   These two have no respect.

Revelation 11:8-10 And their dead bodies shall lie in the street of the great city, which spiritually is called Sodom and Egypt, where also our Lord was crucified. [9] And they of the people and kindreds and tongues and nations shall see their dead bodies three days and an

half, and shall not suffer their dead bodies to be put in graves. [10] And they that dwell upon the earth shall rejoice over them, and make merry, and shall send gifts one to another; because these two prophets tormented them that dwelt on the earth.

The people of the earth will rejoice when they are killed. These two servants of God are considered trouble makers by the people of the earth. They are not even given a proper burial, but are left to rot in the streets.

D.   These two have a big surprise.

Revelation 11:11-12 And after three days and an half the spirit of life from God entered into them, and they stood upon their feet; and great fear fell upon them which saw them. [12] And they heard a great voice from heaven saying unto them, Come up hither. And they ascended up to heaven in a cloud; and their enemies beheld them.

While the news cameras are focused on their dead bodies, while the people are rejoicing, these two stand up alive. Then these two ascend up to Heaven while the people watch.

IV.   The action of The Tribulation.

       We know that The Tribulation will
       begin just after The Rapture.   In
       this   lesson,   we   will   make   a
       chronological   study   starting   just
       after The Rapture and ending with
       The Second Coming of Christ.

       A.   The peaceful period.

             Several of these events will
             transpire simultaneously.

             1.   The   appearance   of   the
                   antichrist.

                   While it is very possible
                   that   the   antichrist   is
                   alive and working in the
                   world right now, he will
                   not begin his work until
                   after The Rapture.

                   **Daniel 11:36-45   And the
                   king   shall   do   according
                   to his will; and he shall
                   exalt   himself,   and
                   magnify   himself   above
                   every   god,   and   shall
                   speak   marvellous   things
                   against the God of gods,
                   and   shall   prosper   till
                   the   indignation   be
                   accomplished: for that
                   that is determined shall
                   be   done.   [37] Neither
                   shall he regard the God
                   of his fathers, nor the
                   desire   of   women,   nor**

regard any god: for he shall magnify himself above all. [38] But in his estate shall he honour the God of forces: and a god whom his fathers knew not shall he honour with gold, and silver, and with precious stones, and pleasant things. [39] Thus shall he do in the most strong holds with a strange god, whom he shall acknowledge and increase with glory: and he shall cause them to rule over many, and shall divide the land for gain. [40] And at the time of the end shall the king of the south push at him: and the king of the north shall come against him like a whirlwind, with chariots, and with horsemen, and with many ships; and he shall enter into the countries, and shall overflow and pass over. [41] He shall enter also into the glorious land, and many countries shall be overthrown: but these shall escape out of his hand, even Edom, and Moab, and the chief of the children of Ammon. [42] He shall stretch forth his hand also upon the countries: and the land of Egypt shall not escape. [43] But he shall have power over the treasures of gold and of silver, and over all of the precious things of Egypt: and the Libyans and the Ethiopians shall be at his steps. [44] But tidings out of the east and out of the north shall trouble him: therefore he shall go forth with great fury to destroy, and utterly to make away many. [45] And he shall plant the tabernacles of his palace between the seas in the glorious holy mountain; yet he shall come to his end, and none shall help him.

1. He will, no doubt, be one of the most dynamic persons of all time possessing great genius in many areas. This genius will be in such areas as economics, politics, military tactics and even religions.

    II Thessalonians 2:3,4,9 Let no man deceive you by any means: For that day shall not come, except there come a falling away first, and that man of sin be revealed, the son of perdition; [4] Who opposeth and exalteth himself above all that is called God, or that is worshipped; so that he as God sitteth in the temple of God, shewing himself that he is God. [9] Even him, whose coming is after the working of Satan with all power and signs and lying wonders.

2. The antichrist will make a peace treaty with Israel that is suppose to last seven years. Of course this treaty will be broken about half way through the Tribulation.

Daniel 9:27 And he shall confirm the covenant with many for one week: and in the midst of the week he shall cause the sacrifice and the oblation to cease, and for the overspreading of abominations he shall make it desolate, even until the consummation, and that determined shall be poured upon the desolate.

3.   During this time the
     great lie will be told to
     explain The Rapture and
     it will be believed. The
     people will want some
     explanation so bad they
     will accept a lie. The
     lie will produce a
     temporary calmness. They
     will experience a short
     peaceful time during the
     first part of The
     Tribulation. I call this
     the calm before the
     storm.

B.   The Pouring out of the Seals.

1.   The First Seal.

     **Revelation 6:2 And I
     saw, and behold a white
     horse: and he that sat
     on him had a bow; and a
     crown was given unto him:
     and he went forth
     conquering, and to
     conquer.**

     What we see here is the
     first part of The
     Tribulation as the
     antichrist comes on the
     scene. He conquers with
     a bow, the arrows are not
     mentioned. He gives the
     appearance of good and
     Godly. Notice the white
     horse. This means he
     will subdue the kingdoms

with his words, no bloodshed at this time. This is when the covenant is made with Israel, and great promises are extended to the rest of the world.

2.   The Second Seal.

Revelation 6:3-4   And when he had opened the second seal, I heard the second beast say, Come and see. [4] And there went out another horse that was red: and power was given to him that sat thereon to take peace from the earth, and that they should kill one another: and there was given unto him a great sword.

Just as the white horse represents a time of peace, the red horse represents a time of bloodshed. This rider carries a sword and has the power to take away peace. War will prevail with people killing one another in a horrible time of bloodshed.

3.   The Third Seal.

Revelation 6:5-6   And when he had opened the third seal, I heard the third beast say, Come and see.   And I beheld, and lo a black horse; and he that sat on him had a pair of balances in his hand.   [6] And I heard a voice in the midst of the four beasts say,   A measure of wheat for a penny, and three measures of barley for a penny; and see thou hurt not the oil and the wine.

The black horse follows the red.   As the bloodshed of the red horse happens, the food supply is neglected.   And now famine, represented by the black horse, follows the red.   Notice the phrase a measure of wheat for a penny and three measures of barley for a penny.   A penny was an entire days wages. Things will be so bad, food will be so expensive that it will take a full day's wages to buy one quart of wheat.   The oil or wine is not harmed.   I believe that the rich will just get richer as

well as fewer in number
while the middle class
disappears into the poor.

4.   The Fourth Seal.

**Revelation 6:7–8 And
when he had opened the
fourth seal, I heard the
voice of the fourth beast
say, Come and see. [8]
And I looked, and behold
a pale horse: and his
name that sat on him was
Death, and Hell followed
with him. And power was
given unto them over the
fourth part of the earth,
to kill with sword, and
with hunger, and with
death, and with the
beasts of the earth.**

This horse is pale in
color and the rider's
name is death. Following
this horse and rider is
hell. These have power
over a forth part of the
earth to kill. Can you
imagine one forth of the
population dying from war
and famine. This will
happen. In other words,
if the population of the
earth is four billion
after The Rapture, one
billion will be killed
during this war and

famine. One out of four
will die.

5. The Fifth Seal.

**Revelation 6:9—11   And
when he had opened the
fifth seal, I saw under
the altar the souls of
them that were slain for
the word of God, and for
the testimony which they
held: [10] And they cried
with a loud voice,
saying, How long, O Lord,
holy and true, dost thou
not judge and avenge our
blood on them that dwell
on the earth?   [11] And
white robes were given
unto every one of them;
and it was said unto
them, that they should
rest yet for a little
season, until their
fellowservants also and
their brethren, that
should be killed as they
were, should be
fulfilled.**

John sees here the
martyrs under the altar.
I believe that these are
those who refused the
mark of the beast. They
have endured until the
end having been slain
because of their faith in
God.   They are given

white robes and are told to rest for a little season. These will have believed the message of the 144,000. Which we studied earlier.

6.   The Sixth Seal.

Revelation 6:12-17 And I beheld when he had opened the sixth seal, and, lo, there was a great earthquake; and the sun became black as sackcloth of hair, and the moon became as blood; [13] And the stars of heaven fell unto the earth, even as a fig tree casteth her untimely figs, when she is shaken of a mighty wind.   [14] And the heaven departed as a scroll when it is rolled together;   and every mountain and island were moved out of their places.   [15] And the kings of the earth, and the great men, and the rich men, and the chief captains, and the mighty men, and every bondman, and every free man, hid themselves in the dens and in the rocks of the mountains. [16] And said to the mountains and rocks, Fall on us, and

hide us from the face of him that sitteth on the throne, and from the wrath of the Lamb: [17] For the great day of his wrath is come; and who shall be able to stand?

There will be many physical changes as the sun becomes black and the moon red and the earth shakes. It is during this time that men will run to the mountains and rocks looking for any place to hide. There will be no hiding places from the wrath of the Lamb.

7.   The Seventh Seal.

Revelation 8:1 And when he had opened the seventh seal, there was silence in heaven about the space of half an hour.

As this seventh seal is opened, an unusual thing happens, silence is in Heaven. This is a pause or a time of preparation for further judgment to fall. At the end of verse five, we see the thunder and lightening of approaching judgment. In verse six, seven angels prepare to sound the trumpets.

C.   The Seven Trumpets Sound.

1.   The First Trumpet Sounds.

Revelation 8:7 The first angel sounded, and there followed hail and fire mingled with blood, and they were cast upon the earth: and the third part of trees was burnt up, and all green grass was burnt up.

I believe this will be literally fulfilled in ice, fire and blood falling from above. As a result, one third of the trees and all the grass is burned.

2.   The Second Trumpet Sounds.

Revelation 8:8-9 And the second angel sounded, and as it were a great mountain burning with fire was cast into the sea: and the third part of the sea became blood; [9] And the third part of the creatures which were in the sea, and had life, died; and the third part of the ships were destroyed.

This could be a flaming meteor that falls into the sea. Considering the area, it is probably the Mediterranean. As a result, one third of the marine life is destroyed. The blood of all these dead creatures turns one third of the sea to blood. Also one third of the ships are destroyed.

3.   The Third Trumpet Sounds.

Revelation 8:10-11   And the third angel sounded, and there fell a great star from heaven, burning as it were a lamp, and it fell upon the third part of the rivers, and upon the fountains of waters; [11] And the name of the star is called Wormwood: and the third part of the waters became wormwood; and many men died of the waters, because they were made bitter.

This is possibly another meteor which falls upon the earth and contaminates the fresh water. It will cause the drinking water to become bitter and again many people die.

4.   The Fourth Trumpet Sounds.

Revelation 8:12-13 And the fourth angel sounded, and the third part of the sun was smitten, and the third part of the moon, and the third part of the stars; so as the third part of them was darkened, and the day shone not for a third part of it, and the night likewise. [13] And I beheld, and heard an angel flying through the midst of heaven, saying with a loud voice, Woe, woe, woe, to the inhabiters of the earth by reason of the other voices of the trumpet of the three angels, which are yet to sound!

As this trumpet sounds the sun, moon and stars are smitten and the daylight hours are cut by one third.

5.   The Fifth Trumpet Sounds.

Revelation 9:1-6 And the fifth angel sounded, and I saw a star fall from heaven unto the earth: and to him was given the key of the bottomless pit. [2] And he opened

the bottomless pit; and
there arose a smoke out
of the pit, as the smoke
of a great furnace; and
the sun and the air were
darkened by reason of the
smoke of the pit. [3]
And there came out of the
smoke locusts upon the
earth: and unto them was
given power, as the
scorpions of the earth
have power. [4] And it
was commanded them that
they should not hurt the
grass of the earth,
neither any green thing,
neither any tree; but
only those men which have
not the seal of God in
their foreheads. [5] And
to them it was given that
they should not kill
them, but that they
should be tormented five
months: and their
torment was as the
torment of a scorpion,
when he striketh a man.
[6] And in those days
shall men seek death and
shall not find it; and
shall desire to die, and
death shall flee from
them.

When this pit is opened,
these demon-like locusts
come out. For five
months these terrible

creatures torture the men that have not the Seal of God. Notice the description of these creatures.

Revelation 9:7-10 And the shapes of the locusts were like unto horses prepared unto battle; and on their heads were as it were crowns like gold, and their faces were as the faces of men. [8] And they had hair as the hair of women, and their teeth were as the teeth of lions. [9] and they had breastplates, as it were breastplates of iron; and the sound of their wings was as the sound of chariots of many horses running to battle. [10] And they had tails like unto scorpions, and there were stings in their tails: and their power was to hurt men five months.

6. The Sixth Trumpet Sounds.

Revelation 9:13-16 And the sixth angel sounded, and I heard a voice from the four horns of the golden altar which is before God, [14] Saying to the sixth angel which

had the trumpet, Loose the four angels which are bound in the great river Euphrates. [15] And the four angels were loosed, which were prepared for an hour, and a day, and a month, and a year, for to slay the third part of men. [16] And the number of the army of the horsemen were two hundred thousand thousand: and I heard the number of them.

There are four demons released from the river Euphrates, and these four lead a demonic army numbering 200 million. Notice the description of these.

Revelation 9:17 And thus I saw the horses in the vision, and them that sat on them, having breastplates of fire, and of jacinth, and brimstone: and the heads of the horses were as the heads of lions; and out of their mouths issued fire and smoke and brimstone.

This army will kill one third of the men by fire and smoke and brimstone which comes out of their mouths.

Revelation 9:18 By these three was the third part of men killed, by the fire, and by the smoke, and by the brimstone, which issued out of their mouths.

Earlier we saw one forth of the people killed; now we see one third killed. I believe it is safe to assume that at least half of the population of the earth will die during the last half of The Tribulation. Thank God, I will be in Heaven.

7.   The Seventh Trumpet Sounds.

Revelation 11:15-19 And the seventh angel sounded; and there were great voices in heaven, saying, The kingdoms of this world are become the kingdoms of our Lord, and of his Christ; and he shall reign for ever and ever. [16] And the four and twenty elders, which sat before God on their seats, fell upon their faces, and worshipped God, [17] Saying, We give

thee thanks, O Lord God Almighty, which art, and wast, and art to come; because thou hast taken to thee thy great power, and hast reigned. [18] And the nations were angry, and thy wrath is come, and the time of the dead, that they should be judged, and that thou shouldest give reward unto thy servants the prophets, and to the saints, and them that fear thy name, small and great; and shouldest destroy them which destroy the earth. [19] And the temple of God was opened in heaven, and there was seen in his temple the ark of his testament: and there were lightnings, and voices, and thunderings, and an earthquake, and great hail.

At the sounding of this trumpet, an announcement is made that the Lord Jesus Christ is soon going to reign forever on earth. At this announcement, those in Heaven rejoice, and the inhabitants of the earth are angry. This seventh trumpet leads to the

93

opening of the seven
vials.

D.   The Seven Vial Judgments.

**Revelation 16:1-21 And I heard
a great voice out of the temple
saying to the seven angels, Go
your ways, and pour out the
vials of the wrath of God upon
the earth.**

1.   The First Vial Judgment.

**Revelation 16:2 And the
first went, and poured
out his vial upon the
earth; and there fell a
noisome and grievous sore
upon the men which had
the mark of the beast,
and upon them which
worshipped his image.**

These sores that fall
upon the followers of the
antichrist will no doubt
be worse than cancer or
anything that we
encounter today. The
only real comparison is
found in the sixth plague
in Egypt during the
Exodus.

**Exodus 9:8-12 And the
Lord said unto Moses and
unto Aaron, Take to you
handfuls of ashes of the
furnace, and let Moses**

sprinkle it toward the heaven in the sight of Pharaoh. [9] And it shall become small dust in all the land of Egypt, and shall be a boil breaking forth with blains upon man, and upon beast, throughout all the land of Egypt. [10] And they took ashes of the furnace, and stood before Pharaoh; and Moses sprinkled it up toward heaven; and it became a boil breaking forth with blains upon man and upon beast. [11] And the magicians could not stand before Moses because of the boils; for the boil was upon the magicians, and upon all the Egyptians. [12] And the Lord hardened the heart of Pharaoh, and he hearkened not unto them; as the Lord had spoken unto Moses.

2.   The Second Vial Judgment.

Revelation 16:3 And the second angel poured out his vial upon the sea; and it became as the blood of a dead man: and every living soul died in the sea.

During the second trumpet, one third of the sea becomes blood. Now during the second vial the entire sea becomes blood, and all life in the sea is completely extinguished. I don't think that even the most vivid imaginations can imagine a sea of blood, with literally thousands of decaying marine life floating on top of the water.

3.   The Third Vial Judgment.

Revelations 16:4 And the third angel poured out his vial upon the rivers and fountains of waters; and they became blood.

In this vial judgment the fresh waters become blood. During the third trumpet judgment one third of the fresh water was made bitter. Now the fresh water becomes blood. There is no doubt the vengeance belongeth to the Lord, and verse six of this sixteenth chapter seems to indicate the vengeance is taken. In Revelation Chapter six and verse ten the martyred ask for their blood to be avenged. The fact that the drinking water becomes blood answers the cry from the martyrs.

4.   The Fourth Vial Judgment.

Revelation 16:8-9   And the fourth angel poured out his vial upon the sun; and power was given unto him to scorch men with fire. [9] And men were scorched with great heat and blasphemed the name of God, which hath power over these plagues: and they repented not to give him glory.

During this vial judgment, you might say that the heat is turned up. Just going outside will result in sunburn beyond our comprehension. Notice the last part of verse nine, "They repented not to give him glory." There are some who will never turn to the Lord regardless of what transpires.

5.   The Fifth Vial Judgment.

Revelation 16:10-11   And the fifth angel poured out his vial upon the

seat of the beast; and his kingdom was full of darkness; and they gnawed their tongues for pain, [11] And blasphemed the God of heaven because of their pains and their sores, and repented not of their deeds.

This vial is directed to the ungodly leaders of this terrible time. These leaders actually chew their tongues because of the pain. Yet they, too, fail to repent and glorify God.

6.   The Sixth Vial Judgment.

Revelation 16:12-16 And the sixth angel poured out his vial upon the great river Euphrates; and the water thereof was dried up, that the way of the kings of the east might be prepared. [13] And I saw three unclean spirits like frogs come out of the mouth of the dragon, and out of the mouth of the beast, and out of the mouth of the false prophet. [14] For they are the spirits of devils, working miracles, which go forth unto the kings of the earth and of

the whole world, to
gather them to the battle
of that great day of God
Almighty. [15] Behold, I
come as a thief. Blessed
is he that watcheth, and
keepeth his garments lest
he walk naked, and they
see his shame. [16] And
he gathered them together
into a place called in
the Hebrew tongue
Armageddon.

During this time this
mighty line that has
divided the countries of
the east and west of that
area since the dawn of
time is dried up. This
1780 mile river that is
1200 yards wide in places
dries up so that the
armies can make their way
to a place called
Armageddon. The
countries will be
deceived and drawn to
Armageddon by three frog
like demons that work
miracles by the power of
Satan.

7. The Seventh Vial
Judgment.

Revelation 16:17-21 And
the seventh angel poured
out his vial into the
air; and there came a

great voice out of the temple of heaven, from the throne, saying, It is done. [18] And there were voices, and thunders, and lightnings; and there was a great earthquake, such as was not since men were upon the earth, so mighty an earthquake, and so great. [19] And the great city was divided into three parts, and the cities of the nations fell: and great Babylon came in remembrance before God, to give unto her the cup of the wine of the fierceness of his wrath. [20] And every island fled away, and the mountains were not found. [21] And there fell upon men a great hail out of heaven, every stone about the weight of a talent: and men blasphemed God because of the plague of the hail; for the plague thereof was exceeding great.

In this vial judgment the words "It is done" are very significant. This is the final vial bringing to a close the worst judgments ever poured out on this earth.

The most catastrophic earthquake of all time shakes the earth. This earthquake may actually move continents.

THE SECOND COMING

No words are adequate for the introduction of The Second Coming of Christ to the earth. This is, no doubt, one of the greatest events on God's calendar. There is no song, no poem, no news article available that can describe the glory and power of that day. As we approach this subject, keep in mind that the church was raptured seven years earlier, and this is the close of The Tribulation. The Second Coming is the bridge between The Tribulation and The Millennial. The Second Coming is what takes the worst of times to one of the best of times. The Second Coming is when Jesus will personally come to this earth the second time. He will not come to be denied and crucified but as King of Kings and Lord of Lords.

With this in mind, let us now study the second coming of our Lord Jesus Christ.

I.   Drum Roll.

In our world today when a great personality is about to come on the scene, he is preceded by a drum roll. This builds the anticipation of the audience, as they eagerly await the appearance of their star.

Just before the greatest person steps onto the world's stage, he is preceded by more than just a drum roll.

St. Matthew 24:29 Immediately after the tribulation of those days

shall the sun be darkened, and the moon shall not give her light, and the stars shall fall from heaven, and the powers of heaven shall be shaken.

St. Luke 21:25   And there shall be signs in the sun, and in the moon, and in the stars; and upon the earth distress   of   nations,   with perplexity; the sea and the waves roaring;

St. Luke 21:26 Men's hearts failing them for fear, and for looking after those things which are coming on the earth: for the powers of heaven shall be shaken.

There is no doubt that all of this activity in the sky will have caused much attention to be focused there.

II.   Dazzling Appearance.

Revelation   19:11-13   And   I   saw heaven opened, and behold a white horse; and he that sat upon him was called Faithful and True, and in righteousness he doth judge and make war.   [12] His eyes were as a flame of fire, and on his head were many crowns; and he had a name written, that no man knew, but he himself. [13] And he was clothed with a vesture dipped in blood; and his name is called The Word of God.

The curtain does not fold back, but the actual heavens open, and the

King of Kings bursts onto the scene with his eyes consuming all the activity of earth's inhabitants, and upon his head the royal diadem. This time Jesus is not clothed with humility and riding upon a colt. This time he is clothed to war against unrighteousness. This time he is riding the victorious white horse.

Revelation 19:14 And the armies which were in heaven followed him upon white horses, clothed in fine linen, white and clean.

And behind this faithful and true rider are all the Saints clothed in fine linen, white and clean, also riding upon this special horse from Heaven to earth.

What a sight, what a sight to see! If you are saved, you will be one of those Saints with him, and you will have the bird's eye view from your white horse.

Jude 14—15 And Enoch also, the seventh from Adam, prophesied of these, saying, Behold, the Lord cometh with ten thousands of his saints. [15] To execute judgment upon all, and to convince all that are ungodly among them of all their ungodly deeds which they have ungodly committed, and of all their hard speeches which ungodly sinners have spoken against him.

However, even all of the unsaved will view the spectacular appearance.

Revelation 1:7   Behold, he cometh with clouds; and every eye shall see him, and they also which pierced him: and all kindreds of the earth shall wail because of him, Even so, Amen.

St. Matthew 24:30   And then shall appear the sign of the Son of man in heaven: and then shall all the tribes of the earth mourn, and they shall see the Son of man coming in the clouds of heaven with power and great glory.

There is no doubt that all the news agencies will have their cameras focused on the coming King, and every one on this earth will view the second coming of Jesus.

III. Down to Earth.

Up to this point Jesus has appeared but still has not set foot on the earth. We know that Jesus will set foot on the Mount of Olives.

Zechariah 14:3-4   Then shall the Lord go forth, and fight against those nations, as when he fought in the day of battle. [4] And his feet shall stand in that day upon the mount of Olives, which is before Jerusalem on the east, and the mount of Olives shall cleave in the midst

thereof toward the east and toward the west, and there shall be a very great valley; and half of the mountain shall remove toward the north, and half of it toward the south.

I was privileged to stand upon the Mount of Olives not too long ago. I remember looking around and thinking this is where he ascended from and also where he will come back to. In that day the Mount of Olives shall split right down the middle. This earthquake seems to be the finale of Christ's Second Coming to the earth. We have had the drum roll, the dazzling appearance, and now Jesus touching down to earth on the Mount of Olives. Now it is time to get down to business. And as we move on to the next section, that is what Jesus does.

IV. Delivering the Jews.

During The Tribulation the Jews will be persecuted more than any other time in history. Because of this persecution, many will flee for refuge in Edom.

After touching down on the Mount of Olives, Jesus will proceed to Edom to gather these Jews from their hiding place. Many believe that the hiding place will be Petra. While this is not specified in the Bible, Petra does fit some basic requirements that would be needed.

Petra is located among cliffs that would be easily defended by a small group. Petra is also a preserved city, no one lives there, but the caves seem to be just waiting for the arrival of tenants. Here at Petra is where the Jews as a whole recognize and accept Jesus. Let us notice some of the Bible verses that have led us to these conclusions.

Revelation 12:6 And the woman fled into the wilderness, where she hath a place prepared of God, that they should feed her there a thousand two hundred and threescore days.

Zachariah 12:10—12 And I will pour upon the house of David, and upon the inhabitants of Jerusalem, the spirit of grace and of supplications: and they shall look upon me whom they have pierced, and they shall mourn for him, as one mourneth for his only son, and shall be in bitterness for him, as one that is in bitterness for his firstborn. [11] In that day shall there be a great mourning in Jerusalem, as the mourning of Hadadrimmon in the valley of Megiddon. [12] And the land shall mourn, every family apart; the family of the house of David apart, and their wives apart; the family of the house of Nathan apart, and their wives apart;

Zechariah 13:6 And one shall say unto him, What are these wounds in

thine hands? Then he shall answer, Those with which I was wounded in the house of my friends.

Amos 9:14-15 And I will bring again the captivity of my people of Israel, and they shall build the waste cities, and inhabit them; and they shall plant vineyards, and drink the wine thereof; they shall also make gardens, and eat the fruit of them. [15] And I will plant them upon their land, and they shall no more be pulled up out of their land which I have given them, saith the Lord thy God.

St. Matthew 14:31 And he shall send his angels with a great sound of a trumpet, and they shall gather together his elect from the four winds, from one end of heaven to the other.

So now we have the King, the Saints with him, along with a large group of Jews marching toward the Valley of Mequildo for a battle. Let us go there also in our next section of study.

V.   Defeat at Armageddon.

Revelation 19:19 And I saw the beast, and the kings of the earth, and their armies, gathered together to make war against him that sat on the horse, and against his army.

Revelation 16:16 And he gathered them together into a place called in the Hebrew tongue Armageddon.

Zechariah 14:1-3 Behold, the day of the Lord cometh, and thy spoil shall be divided in the midst of thee. [2] For I will gather all nations against Jerusalem to battle, and the city shall be taken, and the houses rifled, and the women ravished; and half of the city shall go forth into captivity, and the residue of the people shall not be cut off from the city. [3] Then shall the Lord go forth, and fight against those nations, as when he fought in the day of battle.

We have the largest army ever assembled, gathered together in a place called Armageddon. Satan is the head of this mighty army, and they are set to go against the rider of the horse.

A.   Action.

This could very well be the only war in history with no casualties on the winning side. The losing side will suffer complete defeat. This defeat will not come because of tanks, guns or even the atomic bomb. This defeat comes by the sword that goeth out of the mouth of Jesus. This is truly the power of his Word. When God said, "Let there be light," there was

light. It is by this same
power that Jesus will win the
battle of Armageddon. There is
a verse in St. John that may
give a small glimpse of how
this will happen.

**St. John 18:6 As soon then as
he had said unto them, I am he,
they went backward, and fell to
the ground.**

I believe that when Jesus
speaks and the armies realize
who they are up against, they
will turn on themselves. The
armies of the beast will be
confused and trembling.

**Zechariah 12:2 Behold, I will
make Jerusalem a cup of
trembling unto all the people
round about, when they shall be
in the siege both against Judah
and against Jerusalem.**

The very light of Christ will
produce blindness in animals
and madness in men.

**II Thessalonians 2:8 And then
shall that Wicked be revealed,
whom the Lord shall consume
with the spirit of his mouth,
and shall destroy with the
brightness of his coming.**

**Zechariah 12:4 In that day,
saith the Lord, I will smite
every horse with astonishment,**

and his rider with madness: and I will open mine eyes upon the house of Judah, and will smite every horse of the people with blindness.

The followers of the beast will riot and actually defeat themselves.

B.   Results of this battle.

   1.   Blood will run bridle deep to a horse in an area about 200 miles long.

        Revelation 14:18-20   And another angel came out from the altar, which had power over fire; and cried with a loud cry to him that had the sharp sickle, saying, Thrust in thy sharp sickle, and gather the clusters of the vine of the earth; for her grapes are fully ripe. [19] And the angel thrust in his sickle into the earth, and gathered the vine of the earth, and cast it into the great winepress of the wrath of God. [20] And the winepress was trodden without the city, and blood came out of the winepress, even unto the horse bridles, by the space of a thousand and six hundred furlongs.

2.   All of these dead rotting bodies will become a feast for the birds.

Revelation 19:17-18 And I saw an angel standing in the sun; and he cried with a loud voice, saying to all the fowls that fly in the midst of heaven, Come and gather yourselves together unto the supper of the great God; [18] That ye may eat the flesh of kings, and the flesh of captains, and the flesh of mighty men, and the flesh of horses, and of them that sit on them, and the flesh of all men, both free and bond, both small and great.

Revelation 19:21 And the remnant were slain with the sword of him that sat upon the horse, which sword proceeded out of his mouth; and all the fowls were filled with their flesh.

3.   The beast and the false prophet are cast alive into the lake of fire burning with brimstone.

Revelation 19:20 And the beast was taken, and with him the false prophet that wrought miracles before him, with which he deceived them that had received the mark of the beast, and them that worshipped his image. These both were cast alive into a lake of fire burning with brimstone.

VI. Dividing the Nations.

St. Matthew 25:31-46 When the son of man shall come in his glory, and all the holy angels with him, then shall he sit upon the throne of his glory: [32] And before him shall be gathered all nations: and he shall separate them one from another, as a shepherd divideth his sheep from the goats: [33] And he shall set the sheep on his right hand, but the goats on his left. [34] Then shall the King say unto them on his right hand, Come ye blessed of my Father, inherit the kingdom prepared for you from the foundation of the world; [35] For I was an hungered, and ye gave me meat: I was thirsty, and ye gave me drink: I was a stranger, and ye took me in: [36] Naked, and ye clothed me: I was sick, and ye visited me: I was in prison, and ye came unto me. [37] Then shall the righteous answer him, saying, Lord, when saw we thee an hungered, and fed thee? or thirsty, and gave thee drink? [38] When saw we thee a stranger and took thee in? Or naked, and clothed thee? [39] Or when saw we thee sick, or in prison, and came unto thee? [40] And the King shall answer and say unto them, Verily I say unto you, Inasmuch as ye have done it unto one of the least of these my brethren, ye have done it unto me. [41] Then shall he say also unto them on the left hand, Depart from me, ye cursed, into everlasting fire, prepared for the devil and his angels: [42] For I was hungered, and ye gave me no meat: I was thirsty, and ye gave me no drink: [43] I was a stranger and ye took me not in: naked, and ye clothed me not: sick, and in prison, and ye visited me not. [44] Then shall they also answer him, saying, Lord, when saw we thee an hungered or athirst, or a stranger, or naked, or sick, or in prison, and did not minister unto thee? [45] Then shall he answer them, saying, Verily I say unto you, Inasmuch as ye did it not to one of the least of these, you did it not to me. [46] And these shall go away into everlasting punishment: but the righteous into life eternal.

Some have tried to say that this sheep and goat judgment as it is sometimes called is the same as the Great White Throne Judgment. This is not the case. This sheep and goat judgment is a separate judgment that happens at the Second Coming.

A.   Action.

At this judgment all nations
are brought before the King.
The word nations in the greek
ethics means gentiles or
people. The people that have
survived the Tribulation are
brought before the King for
judgment.

B.   Results.

1.   The wicked who have
survived the Tribulation
will not be allowed to
enter the Millennial
reign. They are
sentenced to follow the
beast and false prophet
into the lake of fire.

**St. Matthew 25:41 Then
shall he say also unto
them on the left hand,
Depart from me, ye
cursed, into everlasting
fire, prepared for the
devil and his angels;**

2.   Those who have endured
until the end without
receiving the mark of the
beast are allowed to
enter the Millennium.

**St. Matthew 25:34 Then
shall the king say unto
them on his right hand,
Come, ye blessed of**

my Father, inherit the kingdom prepared for you from the foundation of the world.

It is important to realize that those people enter the Millennium in their natural bodies.

VII. Dealing with Fallen Angels.

The Bible teaches that we shall judge angels.

I Corinthians 6:3 Know ye not that we shall judge angels? how much more things that pertain to this life?

We now call fallen angels demons. We apparently will not have any problems with the demons during the Millennium, so they must be dealt with before the Millennium starts. That is why we have believed this as time when we shall judge angels.

A good question as a close to this section on the Second Coming would be, how long does all this take? It is very difficult to be dogmatic about many of these things. But we do have some verses that may shed some light on this.

Daniel 12:11-12 And from the time that the daily sacrifice shall be taken away, and the abomination that maketh desolate set up, there shall

117

be a thousand two hundred and ninety days. [12] Blessed is he that waiteth, and cometh to the thousand three hundred and five and thirty days.

There seems to be a forty-five day time period here from the end of the Tribulation to the start of the Millennium. If that is the case, the things that we have just studied will transpire during that time.

THE MILLENNIUM OR 1000 YEAR REIGN OF CHRIST

After the Second Coming of Christ and those events discussed in the last lesson will come the thousand-year reign, also called the Millennial Reign. There is an enormous amount of scripture given to this subject. This lesson will not attempt to make a complete study of the Millennium. What we intend to do is focus on what the Millennium will be like. In order to do this, we must realize that the Millennium is unlike any other time period on earth. This is not Heaven; this is a time when Jesus will rule over the earth. It will be a great time, but even in this time there will be those who will cause problems.

Before we get into our lesson, let us look at the chronological order of the Millennium. First, we have the Rapture, then the Tribulation, followed by the Second Coming and then the Millennium. This view is known as premillennialism.

Now, let us go to the Word of God and learn what the Thousand-Year Reign of Christ will be like.

I.   What will the Millennium be like for Satan?

The Devil has been deceiving people since the Garden of Eden. He is, even today, as a roaring lion seeking whom he may devour. Praise God, during the Millennium the devil will be chained the entire one thousand years.

Revelation 20:1-3 And I saw an angel come down from heaven, having the key of the bottomless pit and a great chain in his hand. [2] And he laid hold on the dragon, that old serpent, which is the Devil, and Satan, and bound him a thousand years, [3] And cast him into the bottomless pit, and shut him up, and set a seal upon him, that he should deceive the nations no more, till the thousand years should be fulfilled: and after that he must be loosed a little season.

Needless to say the Millennium will not be a great time for the devil. The devil will be in the bottomless pit, shut up and sealed. He will not be able to practice deceptions of which he is the father.

John 8:44 Ye are of your father the devil, and the lusts of your father ye will do. He was a murderer from the beginning, and abode not in the truth, because there is no truth in him. When he speaketh a lie, he speaketh of his own: for he is a liar, and the father of it.

II. What will the Millennium be like for the Savior?

The Lord Jesus Christ will be the King of all kings. He will rule the earth during this time. He will have those who rule with him,

121

as we will see later in the lesson. However, David will be ruling as next to the King.

Jeremiah 30:9 But they shall serve the Lord their God, and David their King, whom I will raise up unto them.

As king over all the earth, there will be many areas that Jesus will personally supervise. Jesus will be very busy taking care of these things.

A. Jesus will make sure the Millennium will be a time of peace. Throughout the ages there have been many wars on this earth. The fear of war and the results of war have caused terrible pain to all those involved. There will be peace on earth during this time. It will be when Jesus brings that peace to us.

   Isaiah 2:4 And he shall judge among the nations, and shall rebuke many people: and they shall beat their swords into plowshares, and their spears into pruninghooks: nation shall not lift up sword against nation, neither shall they learn war any more.

   Isaiah 32:17-18 And the work of righteousness shall be peace; and the effect of

righteousness quietness and assurance for ever. [18] And my people shall dwell in a peaceable habitation, and in sure dwellings, and in quiet resting places;

Ezekiel 34:25 And I will make them a covenant of peace, and will cause the evil beasts to cease out of the land: and they shall dwell safely in the wilderness, and sleep in the woods.

Micah 4:2-3 And many nations shall come, and say, Come, and let us go up to the mountain of the Lord, and to the house of the God of Jacob; and he will teach us of his ways, and we will walk in his paths: for the law shall go forth of Zion, and the word of the Lord from Jerusalem. [3] And he shall judge among many people, and rebuke strong nations afar off; and they shall beat their swords into plowshares, and their spears into pruninghooks: nation shall not lift up a sword against nation, neither shall they learn war any more.

Can you imagine living in a time when there will be no wars, no need for a strong military or advanced weapons. This will be the time when they beat their swords into plowshares. The money that usually is spent on weapons will be spent on agriculture. There will be peace through our Lord Jesus Christ.

B. Jesus will make sure that comfort will be provided for everyone. Right now as you read this lesson, someone is broken hearted. Someone has no shoulder to cry on. Someone can't find anywhere to turn for comfort. This will not be true of anyone who follows the path set forth by the King during the Millennium.

Isaiah 12:1 And in that day thou shalt say, O Lord, I will praise thee: though thou wast angry with me, thine anger is turned away, and thou comfortedst me.

Isaiah 51:3 For the Lord shall comfort Zion: he will comfort all her waste places; and he will make her wilderness like Eden, and her desert like the garden of the Lord; joy and gladness shall be found therein, thanksgiving, and the voice of melody.

Isaiah 66:13 As one whom his mother comforteth, so will I comfort you; and ye shall be comforted in Jerusalem.

C.   Jesus will make sure that perfect justice will be administered to each person. Right now we live in the world where justice does not always prevail. There are occasions when the innocent suffer unjustly. There occasions when those guilty of the most terrible crimes go free. Many of the systems that we have to abide by do not always administer justice. During the Millennium, Jesus will make sure that perfect justice will prevail.

Isaiah 9:7 Of the increase of his government and peace there shall be no end, upon the throne of David, and upon his kingdom, to order it, and to establish it with judgment and with justice from henceforth even for ever. The zeal of the Lord of hosts will perform this.

D.   Jesus will make sure there will be no sickness or disease. They that have any deformities will be healed. There will be no blindness, no deafness, no cancer, and no birth defects.

Isaiah 29:17-19 Is it not yet a very little while, and Lebanon shall be turned into a fruitful field, and the fruitful field shall be

esteemed as a forest? **[18] And in that day shall the deaf hear the words of the book, and the eyes of the blind shall see out of obscurity, and out of darkness. [19] The meek also shall increase their joy in the Lord, and the poor among men shall rejoice in the Holy One of Israel.**

Praise the Lord, there will be no need for medical insurance, doctors and hospitals. **Isaiah 65:20** suggests that there will be no dwarfed bodies or those who are mentally handicapped.

E.   Jesus will make sure that proper instructions are given to all people.

Jeremiah 3:14-15   Turn, O backsliding children, saith the Lord; for I am married unto you: and I will take you one of a city, and two of a family, and I will bring you to Zion: [15] And I will give you pastors according to mine heart, which shall feed you with knowledge and understanding.

Micah 4:2   And many nations shall come, and say, Come, and let us go up to the mountain of the Lord, and to the house of the God of Jacob; and he will teach us of his ways, and we

**will walk in his paths: for
the law shall go forth of Zion,
and the word of the Lord from
Jerusalem.**

Lack of knowledge will be a
thing of the past. This full
knowledge will come through the
teaching of the King.

III. What will the Millennium be like
for the Saints?

This often asked question is
difficult to answer. We are curious
about what things are going to be
like for us during the Millennium.

A. We shall ever be with the Lord.

**I Thessalonians 4:17 Then we
which are alive and remain
shall be caught up together
with them in the clouds, to
meet the Lord in the air: and
so shall we ever be with the
Lord.**

At the Rapture we are changed
into new glorified bodies and
told that we shall ever be with
the Lord.

The first thing we need to
understand about our role in
the Millennium is that we will
always be with the Lord. All
else hinges upon this fact.
Many of the areas we studied on
what the Millennium will be

like for the Savior may also apply to the Saints.

B.   We will reign with Christ.

II Timothy 2:11-12   It is a faithful saying: For if we be dead with him, we shall also live with him: [12] If we suffer, we shall also reign with him: if we deny him, he also will deny us:

Revelation 20:4-6   And I saw thrones, and they sat upon them, and judgement was given unto them: and I saw the souls of them that were beheaded for the witness of Jesus, and for the word of God, and which had not worshipped the beast, neither his image, neither had received his mark upon their foreheads, or in their hands; and they lived and reigned with Christ a thousand years.   [5] But the rest of the dead lived not again until the thousand years were finished.   This is the first resurrection.   [6] Blessed and holy is he that hath part in the first resurrection: on such the second death hath no power, but they shall be priests of God and of Christ, and shall reign with him a thousand years.

Revelation 3:21   To him that overcometh will I grant to sit

with me in my throne, even as I also overcame, and am set down with my Father in his throne.

The Saints will actually assist Christ in ruling over the earth. We will help make sure there is peace on earth, that perfect justice is administered, and that proper instructions are taught.

Revelation 2:26-27 And he that overcometh, and keepeth my works unto the end, to him will I give power over the nations: [27] And he shall rule them with a rod of iron; as the vessels of a potter shall they be broken to shivers: even as I received of my Father.

We will rule over saved Israel and the survivors of the Tribulation. I would like to give more details on this area, however, there is limited information on this subject. I guess we will just have to wait until this time comes and then see.

C.   We will worship Christ.

Isaiah 66:23 And it shall come to pass, that from one new moon to another, and from one sabbath to another, shall all flesh come to worship before me, saith the Lord.

Zechariah 14:16 And it shall come to pass, that everyone that is left of all the nations which came against Jerusalem shall even go up from year to year to worship the King, the Lord of hosts, and to keep the feast of tabernacles.

It is possible we will lead the whole world in worship. In closing this area about what the Millennium will be like for the Saints, let us say that Christ will be the center for the Saints. We will be with Christ, reign with Christ, and worship Christ.

IV. What will the Millennium be like for the survivors?

At this point we are talking about those individuals who are allowed to enter the Millennium from the Tribulation. These people will be allowed to enter the Millennium in their natural physical bodies.

A. They will reproduce.

Ezekiel 47:22 And it shall come to pass, that ye shall divide it by lot for an inheritance unto you, and to the strangers that sojourn among you, which shall begat children among you: and they shall be unto you as born in the country among the children

130

of Israel; they shall have inheritance with you among the tribes of Israel.

No doubt the population will soar during the thousand years. These will not only be able to have children, but they may be able to have them during the entire thousand years. Right now a woman's reproductive years are ending while she is in her thirties or forties. During the Millennium, women may be able to have children the full one thousand years.

B. They will suffer punishment. Jesus will rule with the rod. Satan will be gone, but the sin nature will not. Every child that is born will still exhibit the sin nature. This nature will not go unpunished.

Jeremiah 30:20 Their children also shall be as aforetime, and their congregation shall be established before me, and I will punish all that oppress them.

This punishment will be put on display so that all can see the results of transgression.

Isaiah 66:23-24 And it shall come to pass, that from one new moon to another, and from one sabbath to another, shall all

131

flesh come to worship before me, saith the Lord. [24] And they shall go forth, and look upon the carcasses of the men that have transgressed against me: for their worm shall not die, neither shall their fire be quenched; and they shall be an abhorring unto all flesh.

C.   They will labor.

Isaiah 65:21-23 And they shall build houses, and inhabit them; and they shall plant vineyards, and eat the fruit of them. [22] They shall not build, and another inhabit; they shall not plant, and another eat: for as the days of a tree are the days of my people, and mine elect shall long enjoy the work of their hands. [23] They shall not labour in vain, nor bring forth for trouble; for they are the seed of the blessed of the Lord, and their offspring with them.

Houses will be built, farming will provide employment as well as manufacturing. Most all of the things you see made today will be made then, with the exception of arms. This military budget will go to agriculture.

D.   They will be prosperous.

This new society will be free of poverty. There will be no poor, no hunger, and no homeless.

Ezekiel 36:29 I will also save you from all your uncleannesses: and I will call for the corn, and will increase it, and lay no famine upon you.

E. They will all speak one language.

Language barriers will be gone, and once again there will be only one language.

Zephaniah 3:9 For then will I turn to the people a pure language, that they may all call upon the name of the Lord, to serve him with one consent.

V. What will the Millennium be like for the salvaged earth?

During the Tribulation the planet earth suffers a great deal. Even during the fall of man the earth suffered. The earth was cursed because of man's sin.

Genesis 3:17-19 And unto Adam he said, Because thou has hearkened unto the voice of thy wife, and hast eaten of the tree, of which I commanded thee, saying, Thou shalt not

eat of it: cursed is the ground for thy sake; in sorrow shalt thou eat of it all the days of thy life. [18] Thorns, also and thistles shall it bring forth to thee; and thou shalt eat the herb of the field; [19] In the sweat of thy face shalt thou eat bread, till thou return unto the ground, for out of it wast thou taken: for dust thou art, and unto dust shalt thou return.

A.   The earth will be restored, and the original curse lifted.

Amos 9:13 Behold, the days come, saith the Lord, that the plowman shall overtake the reaper, and the treader of grapes him that soweth seed; and the mountains shall drop sweet wind, and all the hills shall melt.

The earth will be able to produce as it did in the Garden of Eden. The roses will have no thorns. The weeds will not choke out the harvest. No spray will be needed, and no chemicals will be needed to prepare the soil. If you think the fruit of the land is good now, just wait till then.

B.   Animal life will be changed.

Isaiah 11:6-9 The wolf also shall dwell with the lamb, and the leopard shall lie down with the kid; and the calf and the young lion and the fatling together; and a little child shall lead them. [7] And the cow and the bear shall feed; their young ones shall lie down together: and the lion shall eat straw like the ox. [8] And the sucking child shall play on the hole of the asp, and the weaned child shall put his hand on the cockatrice' den.

I personally believe that even the meat eating animals will become vegetarians. Men and animals will be living in harmony eating the bounty of the revitalized earth.

VI. What will the Millennium be like for saved Israel?

Israel has been, and still is God's chosen people. They will occupy a different status than others during the Millennium.

A. They will be restored to their first relationship to God.

Isaiah 62:2-5 And the gentiles shall see thy righteousness, and all kings thy glory: and thou shalt be called by a new name, which the mouth of the Lord shall name. [3] Thou

135

shalt also be a crown of glory
in the hand of the Lord, and a
royal diadem in the hand of thy
God. [4] Thou shalt no more be
termed Desolate: but thou
shalt be called Hephzibah, and
thy land Beulah: for the Lord
delighteth in thee, and thy
land shall be married. [5] For
as a young man marrieth a
virgin, so shall thy sons marry
thee; and as the bridegroom
rejoiceth over the bride, so
shall thy God rejoice over
thee.

Many times in Old Testament
scriptures, God refers to
Israel as his unfaithful wife
going after other gods. During
this time, Israel will be
faithful to the one true God.

B.   They will be exalted above the
      gentiles.

      The surviving Israelites will
      hold better positions than the
      surviving gentiles. The
      gentiles will provide services
      for the Jews.

      Isaiah 49:22-23 Thus saith the
      Lord God, Behold, I will lift
      up mine hand to the Gentiles,
      and set up my standard to the
      people: and they shall bring
      thy sons in their arms, and thy
      daughters shall be carried upon
      their shoulders. [23] And

kings shall be thy nursing fathers, and their queens thy nursing mothers: they shall bow down to thee with their face toward the earth, and lick up the dust of thy feet; and thou shalt know that I am the Lord: for they shall not be ashamed that wait for me.

C.   They will become God's witness during the Millennium.

Zephaniah 3:20 At that time will I bring you again, even in the time that I gather you: for I will make you a name and a praise among all people of the earth, when I turn back your captivity before your eyes, saith the Lord.

They may be used in spreading the knowledge of the Lord.

VII. What will the millennium be like for the sanctuary?

We have mentioned worship several times. The place of worship and the way of worship will again be changed.

A.   The temple will again be present during the Millennial.

Isaiah 2:3 And many people shall go and say, Come ye, and let us go up to the mountain of the Lord, to the house of the

God of Jacob; and he will teach us of his ways, and we will walk in his paths: for out of Zion shall go forth the law, and the word of the Lord from Jerusalem.

This is covered in detail in the book of Ezekiel Chapters forty through forty eight.

B. Sacrifices will again take place.

Isaiah 56:6-7 Also the sons of the stranger, that join themselves to the Lord, to serve him, and to love the name of the Lord, to be his servants, every one that keepeth the sabbath from polluting it, and taketh hold of my covenant; [7] Even them will I bring to my holy mountain, and make them joyful in my house of prayer: their burnt offerings and their sacrifices shall be accepted upon mine altar; for mine house shall be called an house of prayer for all people.

Isaiah 60:7 All the flocks of Kedar shall be gathered together unto thee, the rams of Nebaioth shall minister unto thee: they shall come up with acceptance on mine altar, and I will glorify the house of my glory.

In a time of peace, a time when the animals become vegetarians this is a distinctive scene. An animal being killed, the blood drained, the burnt offering upon the altar as a sacrifice.

These sacrifices have a particular purpose. Remember all those children born during this time with that sinful nature. The people, even though they live in the perfect environment, will not automatically be citizens of Heaven. They, too, must receive Jesus Christ. This is the reason the sacrificial system will be present during the Millennium. To show the sacrifice that Jesus made for them, the cost of salvation, and the love of God. Some will accept Christ and some will not.

SATAN'S LAST STAND

We have just studied the Millennial Reign, a time when Satan is bound for the entire one thousand years. Now we are going to briefly study the time after the Millennium, and before the Great White Throne Judgment. We are given little information on this period. So we will take the scriptures that we have and study them.

> **Revelation 20:3   And cast him into the bottomless pit, and shut him up, and set a seal upon him, that he should deceive the nations no more, till the thousand years should be fulfilled: and after that he must be loosed a little season.**

> **Revelation 20:7—10   And when the thousand years are expired, Satan shall be loosed out of his prison, [8] And shall go out to deceive the nations which are in the four quarters of the earth, Gog and Magog, to gather them together to battle: the number of whom is as the sand of the sea.   [9] And they went up on the breadth of the earth, and compassed the camp of the saints about, and the beloved city: and fire came down from God out of heaven, and devoured them. [10] And the devil that deceived them was cast into the lake of fire and brimstone, where the beast and the false prophet are, and shall be tormented day and night for ever and ever.**

I.   The Release.

As we have already studied, Satan
will be imprisoned in a bottomless
pit during the thousand year reign.
However, at the end of this period,
Satan is released.   This is the
deceiver let out to deceive, the
father of lies let out to lie, to
again spread his evil influence
across the earth.

A.   The length of this release.

We are not given a length of
time for this release.   The
Bible only calls it a little
season. There is no doubt that
Satan will work fast and
furious.   The length of this
period will be long enough for
Satan to deceive thousands.

II.   The Reasons.

There have been many who asked the
question, "Why let Satan loose?" He
is bound; why let him go?   I
personally believe there are some
very good answers to this question.

A.   The kingdom children are not
changed.

These that were born during the
Millennium still have the
sinful nature. Even a thousand
years of peace and living under
King Jesus will not erase this
nature.   Man's heart is still

142

desperately wicked. The environment can't change that now and will not change the heart then.

B. God gives man a choice.

Man is a free moral agent and has always been given the opportunity to choose. During the Millennium sacrifices will again be started. The purpose of the sacrifices is to show what Jesus did at Calvary.

When Satan is loosed, he will present his position to the kingdom children, and they will have to make a choice. Some will, no doubt, have believed during the Millennium; others will harden their hearts and wait.

III. The Revolt.

A. Satan's influence will spread like wild fire to all areas of the earth. There will be a tremendous number who will decide to follow Satan. The Bible calls them the number of whom is as the sand of the sea. Many of these who were born during the thousand year reign of Christ and have lived in the perfect environment make the terrible decision to follow Satan.

B.   Satan's influence will cause
them to attempt to overthrow
Christ. Satan has lost many
battles and never seems to
learn.   This is his final
revolt or his final attempt.
This is Satan's last stand.

IV. The Results.

A.   Fire will come down out of
Heaven and devour them. All
that follow Satan will perish
in the final war.

B.   The devil that deceived them
was cast into the lake of fire.
This is the devil's final and
eternal destination. No more
to be loosed, no more to spread
his evil influence. We are
told that Satan will be
tormented day and night for
ever and ever.

**Revelation 20:10 And the devil
that deceived them was cast
into the lake of fire and
brimstone, where the beast and
the false prophet are, and
shall be tormented day and
night for ever and ever.**

GREAT WHITE THRONE JUDGMENT

I. The Judge of the Throne.

II. The Journey to the Throne.

III. The Jury of the Throne.

IV. The Judged of the Throne.

V. The Judgment of the Throne.

VI. The Just of the Throne.

I hope in this study we have annihilated any ideas you may have had of one general judgment. This is the third judgment we have studied. The first was the Bema Judgment where the Christians will stand. The second was the Judgment of the Nations taking place during the second coming of Christ. And now we have the Great White Throne Judgment which is the third judgment. Every man, woman, boy and girl has an appointment to be judged. Rest assured if one hasn't stood before one of the previous judgments, he or she will stand here.

Hebrews 9:27 And as it is appointed unto men once to die, but after this the judgment:

There are two sections of scripture from which we glean much of our information about the Great White Throne Judgment.

Revelation 20:11-15 And I saw a great white throne, and him that sat on it, from whose face the earth and the heaven fled away; and there was found no place for them. [12] And I saw the dead, small and great, stand before God; and the books were opened: and another book was opened, which is the book of life: and the dead were judged out of those things which were written in the books, according to their works. [13] And the sea gave up the dead which were in it; and death and hell delivered up the dead which were in them: and they were judged every

man according to their works. [14] And death and hell were cast into the lake of fire. This is the second death. [15] And whosoever was not found written in the book of life was cast into the lake of fire.

Daniel 7:9-10 I beheld till the thrones were cast down, and the Ancient of days did sit, whose garment was white as snow, and the hair of his head like the pure wool: his throne was like the fiery flame, and his wheels as burning fire. [10] A fiery stream issued and came forth from before him: thousand thousands ministered unto him, and ten thousand times ten thousand stood before him: the judgment was set, and the books were opened.

Let us now make our study of this final judgment.

I.   The Judge of the throne - The Lord Jesus Christ.

In our court systems some judges are fair; others are not. Some judges are lenient; others are harsh. The judge of this bench is perfect and fair. The judge of this bench is none other than the Lord Jesus Christ.

St. John 5:22 For the Father judgeth no man, but hath committed all judgment unto the Son:

St. John 5:27 And hath given him authority to execute judgment also, because he is the Son of man.

Acts 10:40—42 Him God raised up the third day, and shewed him openly; [41] Not to all the people, but unto witnesses chosen before of God, even to us, who did eat and drink with him after he rose from the dead. [42] And he commanded us to preach unto the people, and to testify that it is he which was ordained of God to be the Judge of quick and dead.

II Timothy 4:1 I charge thee therefore before God, and the Lord Jesus Christ, who shall judge the quick and the dead at his appearing and his kingdom;

The very one that the people have rejected will be the one that they stand before. The Way, the Truth and the Life will be the judge.

II. The Journey to the Throne.

I believe that every man, woman, boy and girl that has ever been conceived from the time of Adam until the end of Satan's last stand will be here. However, the believers will be spectators, while the unbelievers will be judged. The journey to the throne will come from every place imaginable. Even the occupants of hell in the center of the earth will be released to journey to the throne.

Revelation 20:13 And the sea gave up the dead which were in it; and death and hell delivered up the dead which were in them: and they were judged every man according to their works.

III. The Jury of this Throne.

In verse twelve of Revelation 20, we read that the books are opened. This is plural meaning more than one. Then we read that another book is opened. This book which has more emphasis placed upon it is the Book of Life. The Bible mentions four other books that may be employed at this throne. The combination of these books will produce a life story of each individual. God is keeping records of the lives of each person. Let us take a look at these five books.

A. The Book of Conscience.

Romans 2:15 Which shew the work of the law written in their hearts, their conscience also bearing witness, and their thoughts the mean while accusing or else excusing one another;

Our conscience may not always be the best guide. However, God put our conscience there to point us in the right direction. Records are being kept, and God is concerned with

149

those times when man goes
against conscience.

B.   The Book of Words.

**St. Matthew 12:36-37 But I say
unto you, That every idle word
that men shall speak, they
shall give account thereof in
the day of judgment. [37] For
by thy words thou shalt be
justified, and by thy words
thou shalt be condemned.**

C.   The Book of Secret Words and
Works.

**Romans 2:16   In the day when
God shall judge the secrets of
men by Jesus Christ according
to my gospel.**

**Ecclesiastes 12:14   For God
shall bring every work into
judgment, with every secret
thing, whether it be good, or
whether it be evil.**

Friend, nothing can be hid from
God, not our words and not our
works.   Not even our secret
thoughts and secret works can
be hid.

D.   The Book of Public Works.

**II Corinthians 11:15 Therefore
it is no great thing if his
ministers also be transformed
as the ministers of**

righteousness; whose end shall be according to their works.

St. Matthew 16:27 For the son of man shall come in the glory of his Father with his angels; and then he shall reward every man according to his works.

Even the lost are judged according to their works. All that are judged here are lost. However, the judgment of their works may determine the degree of punishment in hell. The wicked Adolf Hitler may be given more eternal torments than a morally good man.

E. The Book of Life.

Philippians 4:3 And I intreat thee also, true yokefellow, help those women which laboured with me in the gospel, with Clement also, and with other my fellowlabourers, whose names are in the book of life.

Revelation 20:12 And I saw the dead, small and great stand before God; and the books were opened: and another book was opened which is the book of life: and the dead were judged out of those things which were written in the books, according to their works.

Revelation 21:27   And there shall in no wise enter into it any thing that defileth, neither whatsoever worketh abomination, or maketh a lie: but they which are written in the Lamb's book of life.

The Book of Life is the book of the living. This book records the names of all those who have accepted Christ as Savior. And those who have not accepted Christ as Savior are not written in this book.

IV. The Judged of this Throne.

As we have already mentioned, all those who have never been saved will be judged.

Revelation 20:12   And I saw the dead, small and great, stand before God; and the books were opened: and another book was opened which is the book of life: and the dead were judged out of those things which were written in the books, according to their works.

Regardless of wealth or poverty, power or position, pride or arrogance, they will be judged.

Revelation 20:13 And the sea gave up the dead which were in it; and death and hell delivered up the dead which were in them: and they were

judged every man according to their works.

Even those who have already spent years in hell will be released and judged.

V. The Judgment of the Throne.

Revelation 20:15 And whosoever was not found written in the book of life was cast into the lake of fire.

When the sentence is handed down, it will not be twenty years or life without parole. It will be eternity in the lake of fire.

They are sentenced to eternal death.

Revelation 20:14 And death and hell were cast into the lake of fire. This is the second death.

Death is separation. Death, as we know it now, is separation of soul and spirit from the body.

This second death is the soul and spirit being eternally separated from God. The saved have eternal life and the lost have eternal death.

This eternal death is in the lake of fire.

St. Matthew 8:12 But the children of the kingdom shall be cast out

into outer darkness: there shall be weeping and gnashing of teeth.

St. Matthew 25:30 And cast ye the unprofitable servant into outer darkness: there shall be weeping and gnashing of teeth.

St. Matthew 25:46 And these shall go away into everlasting punishment: but the righteous into life eternal.

Revelation 20:15 And whosoever was not found written in the book of life was cast into the lake of fire.

I believe this lake of fire does not burn with a red flame as we are accustomed to seeing. I don't even believe it burns with a yellow, orange, or blue flame as you may have seen. I believe it burns with a black flame. The unbelievers are cast into a lake burning with a dark black flame. They will only be able to hear the screams of others in agony. They will not be able to see others in the lake of fire. Imagine the torments and the heat and the eternal loneliness of those who are given this sentence.

VI.   The Just (Saved) of the Throne.

We will not be judged here; but we will be spectators. And, yes, this will be a horrible time for all. Seeing those who have rejected Christ receive their sentence. Those we should have witnessed to, those we worked with and lived near sentenced to eternal death. Let us do our job so that their blood will not be required at our hands.

UNTIL

I. The New Earth.

II. The New Heaven.

III. The New Jerusalem.

After the Great White Throne
Judgment, John tells us he saw a New
Heaven and a New Earth. This is the
closing of a time period of this earth as
we know it, and the beginning of a new
and eternal time period. It is also
during this time that we are introduced
to the New Jerusalem. These places the
believers will call home for all
eternity. Let us now take a look at the
New Earth, New Heaven, and New Jerusalem.

I. The New Earth.

**Revelation 21:1 And I saw a new
heaven and a new earth: for the
first heaven and the first earth
were passed away; and there was no
more sea.**

We are told in the scriptures that
there will be a new earth and the
former earth will pass away.

**II Peter 3:10–13 But the day of the
Lord will come as a thief in the
night; in the which the heavens
shall pass away with a great noise,
and the elements shall melt with
fervent heat, the earth also and the
works that are therein shall be
burned up. [11] Seeing then that
all these things shall be dissolved,
what manner of persons ought ye to
be in all holy conversation and
godliness, [12] Looking for and
hasting unto the coming of the day
of God, wherein the heavens being on
fire shall be dissolved, and the
elements shall melt with fervent**

heat?   [13] Nevertheless we, according to his promise, look for new heavens and a new earth, wherein dwelleth righteousness.

There may be some question about the earth as we know it being totally done away with.

My personal opinion is that the new earth will be a fire-washed old earth. We are referred to as a new creature after salvation. However, this new creature came from the old. Let us look at these verses of scripture.

II Peter 3:6 Whereby the world that then was, being overflowed with water, perished:

We are told that the earth that was completely flooded perished. Now, the earth after the flood was the same planet; however, the flood had washed away the people. The conditions were changed. The pre-flood world did not have rain as we know it. The dew came up and provided water. After the flood, things were different. The rain fell.

I believe that instead of using water, God will use fire the next time. This fire will purify the earth creating a new earth. There are three things we want to notice about this new earth.

Ecclesiastes 1:4 One generation passeth away, and another generation cometh: but the earth abideth for ever.

A.   No Sea.

This new earth has no sea. This will create an earth with a great deal more surface area. This earth will be a paradise, a perfect place with the perfect climate.

B.   No Hell.

At the present time hell is in the center of the earth. At the Great White Throne Judgment, the occupants of hell are delivered to the judgment. They are then cast into the lake of fire which is the eternal hell. This is not located in the center of the new earth. It is located in some remote dark place in this universe.

Matthew 25:30 And cast ye the unprofitable servant into outer darkness: there shall be weeping and gnashing of teeth.

C.   No Traces of Sin.

This new earth will have no reminders of sin.

159

Isaiah 65:17   For, behold, I
create new heavens and a new
earth: and the former shall
not be remembered, nor come
into mind.

II.   The New Heaven.

Revelation 21:1   And I saw a new
heaven and a new earth: for the
first heaven and the first earth
were passed away; and there was no
more sea.

Again we need to be clear about what
the scriptures are saying.   The
verse says the first Heaven was
passed away.   If the first Heaven is
the one that passes away, then the
first Heaven must also be the one
that is new.   The Bible teaches us
that there are three Heavens.

A.   The First Heaven.

This is the Heaven of the birds
and clouds - our atmosphere.

Daniel 4:12   The leaves thereof
were fair, and the fruit
thereof much, and in it was
meat for all: the beasts of
the field had shadow under it
and the fowls of the heaven
dwelt in the boughs thereof,
and all flesh was fed of it.

Jeremiah 4:25   I beheld, and,
lo, there was no man, and all

the birds of the heavens were fled.

This is interesting to think about when we realize that the atmosphere that we now have is hurting. Pollution is filling it. The Ozone Layer is thinning and even has holes. This will be the new Heaven. But let us also look at the other two Heavens.

B.   The Second Heaven.

This is the Heaven we now call space where the sun, moon and stars are located.

Genesis 22:17 That in blessing I will bless thee, and in multiplying I will multiply thy seed as the stars of the heaven, and as the sand which is upon the sea shore; and thy seed shall possess the gate of his enemies;

Psalm 19:1 The heavens declare the glory of God; and the firmament sheweth his handywork.

C.   The Third Heaven where God dwells.

II Corinthians 12:2 I knew a man in Christ above fourteen years ago, (whether in the body, I cannot tell; or whether

161

out of the body, I cannot tell; God knoweth;) such an one caught up to the third heaven.

Within this third Heaven exists a glorious holy city called the New Jerusalem. This New Jerusalem is the center of God's presence and will be the home of the believers throughout eternity. This takes us to our next section The New Jerusalem.

III. The New Jerusalem.

Revelation 21:2 And I John saw the holy city, New Jerusalem coming down from God out of heaven, prepared as a bride adorned for her husband.

What a beautiful city this is, but before we take a look at the beauty, let us take a look at what the city is missing.

A.   A City of No Tears.

Revelation 21:4 And God shall wipe away all tears from their eyes; and there shall be no more death, neither sorrow, nor crying, neither shall there be any more pain: for the former things are passed away.

Up until this time there have been rivers of tears shed. But in this city there will be no weeping. I don't believe that

162

we will experience eternity with anything that would cause a tear. When God wipes the tears away, God will also wipe away the thoughts that would bring tears. There will be no painful memories.

Isaiah 65:17 For, behold, I create new heavens and a new earth: for the former shall not be remembered, nor come into mind.

B. A City of No Death.

Revelation 21:4 And God shall wipe away all tears from their eyes; and there shall be no more death, neither sorrow, nor crying, neither shall there be any more pain: for the former things are passed away.

Death has broken many hearts and caused a lot of pain. This is a city of no death.

C. A City of No Sorrow or Pain.

Revelation 21:4 And God shall wipe away all tears from their eyes; and there shall be no more death, neither sorrow, nor crying, neither shall there be any more pain: for the former things are passed away.

A city where there will be no broken homes, abused children, battered wives, traffic accidents, or painful diseases. What a city!

D.   A City of No Night.

Revelation 21:25 And the gates of it shall not be shut at all by day: for there shall be no night.

Zechariah 14:6-7 And it shall come to pass in that day, that the light shall not be clear, nor dark: [7] But it shall be one day which shall be known to the Lord, not day, nor night: but it shall come to pass, that at evening time it shall be light.

This city will experience one eternal day with no death, sorrow, crying, or pain. One eternal day filled with light, joy and the glory of God. Now let us look at some of the cities beauty.

E.   A City of Tremendous Size.

Revelation 21:16 And the city lieth foursquare, and the length is as large as the breadth: and he measured the city with the reed, twelve thousand furlongs. The length and the breadth and the height of it are equal.

Using our present day measurements, this would put the city about 1,500 miles long, wide and high. Most people envision this city shaped as a cube. This is a very large cube which will be suspended in space near the earth.

F.   A City of Unique Foundations.

Revelation 21:19–20 And the foundations of the wall of the city were garnished with all manner of precious stones. The first foundation was jasper; the second, sapphire; the third, a chalcedony; the fourth, an emerald; [20] The fifth, sardonyx; the sixth, sardius; the seventh, chrysolyte; the eighth, beryl; the ninth, a topaz; the tenth, a chrysoprasus; the eleventh, a jacinth; the twelfth, an amethyst.

This will be a very colorful foundation for sure. Let us notice the colors. The first foundation is jasper which is a crystal clear transparent stone. The second foundation is sapphire, a stone which is a blue color. The third is chalcedony which is a sky blue stone often with streaks of other colors. The fourth is emerald, a bright green stone.

The fifth sardonyz which is a white stone with streaks of red. The sixth is sardius, a fiery red. The seventh foundation is a chrysolyte stone, which is yellow gold in color. The eighth is beryl, a sea green stone. The ninth foundation is of topaz, a brownish gold stone. The tenth is chrysoprasus, a blue green stone. The eleventh is a violet stone called jacinth. The twelfth is a purple stone called amethyst.

G.   A City of Jasper Walls.

Revelation 21:17-18   And he measured the wall thereof, an hundred and forty and four cubits, according to the measure of a man, that is, of the angel.   [18] And the building of the wall of it was of jasper: and the city was pure gold, like unto clear glass.

Above these colorful foundations extend jasper walls, walls usually were built for protection. These 216-foot high jasper walls are only for beauty.

H.   A City of Pearly Gates.

Revelation 21:12—13 And had a wall great and high, and had twelve gates, and at the gates twelve angels, and names written thereon, which are the names of the twelve tribes of the children of Israel. [13] On the east three gates; on the north three gates; on the south three gates; and on the west three gates.

These are not merely gates made of pearls, but each gate is of one pearl. This is a huge pearl that people will be able to walk through. There will be three gates on each side of the city making a total of twelve gates. Twelve large pearls for twelve beautiful gates.

I.   A City of the Golden Street.

Revelation 21:21 And the twelve gates were twelve pearls: every several gate was of one pearl: and the street of the city was pure gold, as it were transparent glass.

This is gold that you can see through, transparent like glass. Notice that the word street is not plural. There is only one street in this city. I believe it extends from the bottom to the top like a spiral staircase.

J.   A City of Very Bright Light.

Revelation 21:23 And the city had no need of the sun, neither of the moon, to shine in it: for the glory of God did lighten it, and the Lamb is the light thereof.

Jesus will light up the city. This is, in my opinion, the reason so many of the materials are transparent. Nothing will diminish the brightness and beauty of the Savior.   There will be no shadows, no dark corners, the light of Jesus will illuminate through the entire city.

K.   A City of Pure River and Tree of Life.

Revelation 22:1-2   And he shewed me a pure river of water of life, clear as crystal, proceeding out of the throne of God and of the Lamb.   [2] In the midst of the street of it, and on either side of the river, was there the tree of life, which bare twelve manner of fruits, and yielded her fruit every month: and the leaves of the tree were for the healing of the nations.

We have here the beauty of a pure river clear as crystal. And to go along with this river a wonderful tree of life that bears twelve kinds of fruit. This, no doubt, will be a beautiful sight to behold. I wonder sometimes what other beautiful visions of nature will accompany this park area of the New Jerusalem.

L.   A City of No Temple.

Revelation 21:22 And I saw no temple therein: for the Lord God Almighty and the Lamb are the temple of it.

The temple has always represented the place where people gather to worship. The place of worship in this city is at the feet of Jesus.

IV.   New Locations.

A.   <u>This Holy City</u>, New Jerusalem is right now located in the third Heaven. After the Great White Throne Judgment, this city will come down.

Revelation 21:2 And I John saw the holy city, new Jerusalem, coming down from God out of heaven, prepared as a bride adorned for her husband.

The city's new location will be just above the earth in space.

God will inhabit this city in its new location.

Revelation 21:3 And I heard a great voice out of heaven saying, Behold, the tabernacle of God is with men, and he will dwell with them, and they shall be his people, and God himself shall be with them, and be their God.

B.   The Saints.

The believers will have access to the earth and the holy city. This is the permanent location for all believers.

C.   The Sinners.

Right now, hell is in the heart of the earth, but that will also change locations. The unbelievers will be eternally in the lake of fire.

Revelation 20:15 And whosoever was not found written in the book of life was cast into the lake of fire.

This is Until, the eternal state that the Bible teaches.

Praise the Lord!!! Thank you for reading this book. My desire and prayer is that this book has been a blessing to you in many ways. I trust that FROM THE RAPTURE UNTIL has been a help to you in understanding future events in Bible prophecy.

If you would like to be a blessing to other Christians and a help to this ministry, all you need do is tell others about this book, give them the address to order the book, or better yet, order several copies for your friends. You may even be able to get it into your church as a special Bible Study. There are churches using this book in their Sunday Schools or Bible Study classes.

Again, THANK YOU and PRAISE THE LORD!!!

Please forward _____ books to:

Name: _____
Address: _____
City: _____
State: _____
Zip Code: _____

$9.95 per book plus shipping and handling

EVER-READ PUBLISHING COMPANY
Randy H. Edwards
1675 Pipers Gap Road
Mount Airy, NC 27030
Telephone (919) 786-4805